Essential of Reiki

A Complete Steps From Basic to The Master (revised edition)

Mikao Usui

Based on the teachings of Reiki Master : Mikao Usui

Preface

Reiki is a gift in the form of vitality and self preservation encoded in genes making up of all God's living creatures.

It is the higher self's connection to the universal energy that breathes life into all living things.

We are all born with the omniscient wisdom to heal and preserve life. All living things are connected.

Our ancestors used and relied on their own abilities and instincts.

Unfortunately, these basic skills have been forgotten and are rarely used today.

Humanity in its relentless ambition for progress has given up its most precious and natural gift.

Through the media and clever advertising campaigns the majority of the world's population have been conditioned to rely heavily on modern technology at the expense of their own birthright.

There is a need for humanity to become re-balanced. Instead of giving up responsibility for one's life and health, it is vitally important to regain equilibrium between ancient and modern technology.

Reiki is the catalyst

Many people believe when you are ready to embrace the principles of Reiki you will be guided to a Master.

 I personally believe that Reiki with its infinite wisdom and unconditional love seeks out a person when he or she needs it the most.

This is true according to my own experience and recognition to Reiki.

"Reiki is love, Love is wholeness, Wholeness is balance, Balance is well being, Well being is freedom from disease"

Dr Mikao Usui

Author & Publisher Disclaimer

Reiki is an ancient form of healing that is practised by the author and numerous practitioners around the world.

The information and techniques in this book do not constitute medical advice. Reiki Healing and Medical Healing are two very different disciplines.

You should always remember to seek medical advice from a qualified doctor or practitioner in the case of serious illness.

While all suggested treatments are offered in good faith, the author and publisher are not responsible for any illness arising from the failure by the reader/individual in seeking medical advice from a qualified doctor or medical practitioner.

Important Note for the Readers/Students

The purpose of this book is to provide the reader a comprehensive guide to the teachings and disciplines associated with Usui Reiki.

We have purposely kept the information concise so that the reader can quickly and easily understand and apply Reiki.

Wherever possible we have avoided adding personal beliefs that may differ from the traditional teachings of Dr Mikao Usui.

The knowledge and information contained in this book is based on the original **Shiki Ryoho** Method of Healing developed by **Dr Usui** over two hundred years ago.

In case you want to use the teachings in this book to heal yourself and others, you must first have received the necessary attunements from a Reiki Master either in person or through distant attunement.

Ki & ReiKi

The Universal Life Force Energy

(Chi, Ki, Mana, Prana, Barraka)

Theory of Holistic Healing

To be able to live a healthy life, human does not only need foods and drinks in sufficient quantity, but also needs "Ki".

 Disturbances in the circulation of "Ki" will cause disturbances in "etheric body" followed by pain in the physical body.

Holistic healing works in layers etheric body which indirectly will affect the physical body.

Reiki is a form of hands on healing, with its origins in India and the East dating back thousands of years ago to the time before Christ and Buddha.

 The original name, disciplines and techniques of Reiki were lost due to the traditional method of passing knowledge from one generation to another through word of mouth.

This ancient art of healing is hard to be found because it has long gone

However, we knew that it was rediscovered by a Japanese Scholar and monk , **Dr Mikao Usui**. In fact, Dr Usui was the one who named it **REIKI**.

Reiki is a two syllable Japanese word it means a universal life force.

Although the proper Japanese pronunciation is RYE-KEY, it has been westernised to RAY-KEY.

Rei means universal, omnipresent Esoterically, Rei means spiritual consciousness, the omniscient wisdom from God or the higher self.

Ki is the non physical vitality that gives life to all living things. Many cultures understand and recognise the importance of Ki energy and how it impacts on our lives and well-being.

Ki energy can be activated for the purpose of healing.

When you feel healthy and full of enthusiasm, the flow of Ki energy in your body is high and unencumbered. Life seems easier to deal with and you have a higher resistance to illnesses and diseases.

However, when your Ki energy is low due to stress, feeling unhappy or tired illnesses you will be more vulnerable to diseases.

Your attitude will be generally negative and you will find it difficult to deal with life's challenges.

Ki is the very essence of soul; it leaves the body when a person dies.

Reiki is holistic; it works on the body, mind and spirit by stimulating a person's natural healing abilities.

The blocked emotional and physical elements leading to illness and disease are cleared. Reiki is neither positive nor negative; it is in fact the highest and most profound vibration of life.

Divine in origin, it allows us all to become one with all the living things in our world. Reiki is a pure unconditional love and joy bringing all who experience and embrace its principles together in harmony.

The skills and techniques associated with Reiki are simple and easy to learn. Children and adults can equally comprehend and apply this ancient form of healing into their lives.

Regular contact with Reiki will bring the recipient's mind, body, and spirit into balance. It will also help to prevent illnesses and diseases in the future.

How does Reiki Work?

The human body is made up of over 50 trillion cells. Each cell contains omniscient wisdom and is connected to the universe and every living thing within.

A good analogy is to think of the universe as a huge ocean of water. Every living thing within that ocean is like a tiny droplet.

Together these droplets constitute and are part of Reiki, the universal life force.

Reiki is a part of our genetic structure. An in built intelligence that energises the mind, body, and spirit.

Reiki stimulates growth, health, life and healing. When it is freely allowed to flow around the body it can keep us alive and healthy for over one hundred and twenty years.

Unfortunately, bad habits and poor choices result in the flow of Reiki being stifled. It is important to note that Reiki cannot be destroyed.

Even when we die and the life force leaves our body, it continues to exist as part of the universe. Through neglect and ignorance, we abuse this vital component of life.

When the mind body and spirit are in harmony, the biological intelligence that governs the body's resources and allows it to heal itself and function correctly are intensified.

Reiki is the key that unlocks the body's optimum capabilities. There are seven main energy centres in the body that control the flow of the universal life force. They are called the **Chakras**.

Each chakra is responsible for supplying energy to specific parts of the body.

When they are blocked or clogged, the body becomes sick and the flow of energy is diluted.

A full Reiki treatment reopens the chakras and re-balances the flow of the universal life force around the body. A person will normally need four full treatments on four consecutive days to boost the flow of Reiki energy.

This will stimulate the body's immune system and natural healing abilities. Normally, the body will begin by cleansing itself of toxins. As the poisons are removed, the body becomes re-balanced and the healing process can begin.

Many cultures have developed techniques and disciplines that stimulate the flow of KI energy around the body.

 However, Reiki is the easiest to learn and administer. The techniques are simple to master.

The results are profound.

Main chakras in the Etheric Body System

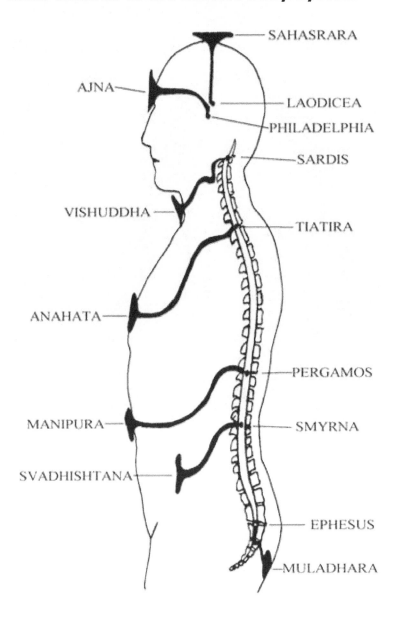

Human Body

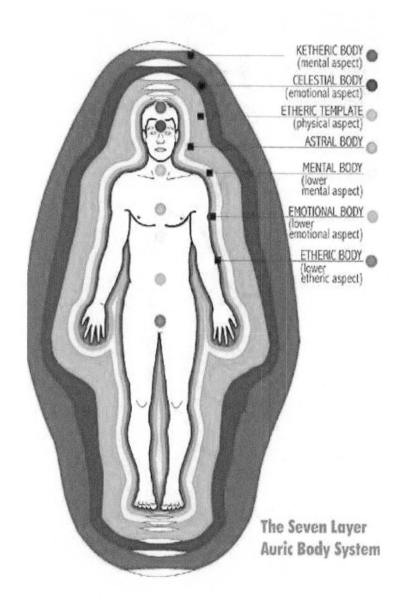

KETHERIC BODY
(mental aspect)

CELESTIAL BODY
(emotional aspect)

ETHERIC TEMPLATE
(physical aspect)

ASTRAL BODY

MENTAL BODY
(lower
mental aspect)

EMOTIONAL BODY
(lower
emotional aspect)

ETHERIC BODY
(lower
etheric aspect)

The Seven Layer
Auric Body System

Reiki-Ho

Sensei Mikao Usui
(1865 – 1926)

Reiki-Ho is an esoteric system that can harness the energy of Reiki optimally for various purposes, including self healing and other healing.

Reiki-Ho was found on 1923 by Sensei Mikao Usui, after his meditating at Mount Kurama, Japan.

Reiki Principles

Reiki Principles

Kyo dake wa
(for today only)

Okoru na
(do not anger)

Shinpai suna
(do not worry)

Kansha shite
(be humble)

Go wo hage me
(be honest in your work)

Hito ni shinsetsu ni
(be compassionate to yourself and others)

The Reiki principles are spiritual ideals.

By adopting these precepts, you will bring balance and substance in your life.

It is important to realise that you are not expected to live every moment of your life within the framework of these ideals.

As humans, we are all imperfect, and that is why each principle begins with "Just for today."

You can't live without pressures or stresses at work, these problems improve your personality every single day.

If you slip up today, you can always begin again tomorrow.

The more you work with the principles, the more you will condition yourself to adopt them as a way of life.

To become more familiar with the Reiki principles, it is advisable to read them aloud at least twice a day. You may wish to place a large copy of the ideals in a picture frame.

Then you could position the copy in a prominent place where you are sure to see it each day, or if you are going to practise Reiki professionally, place it in your healing room.

The Five Reiki principles mean different things to each one of us.

Meditation will help to unlock your own perceptions. Simply sit or lie down in a comfortable position and close your eyes.

Repeat one of the ideals several times aloud using it as a mantra. As you drift into a meditative state you become aware of what is happening inside your mind and body.

You may experience many different feelings, emotions and thoughts.

When you do this exercise in a group share your experiences and write down everything that happened during the meditation.

It is interesting to look at your notes on this exercise on a regular basis to see how you have grown by adopting these precepts.

Repeat the exercise of meditating on each principle annually and compare the notes, if it is conducted in a group setting discuss the differences that have taken place.

Just For Today I Will Not Be Angry

Anger is an emotion.

When we get angry, we lose control of that emotion. In order to live by the above principle we must understand what triggers our anger and how we can choose to remove this destructive emotion from our being.

In every confrontation that leads to anger, the person or thing pushing your anger button has complete power and control over you.

This simple realisation allows you to take back control of your emotions and as such you can now choose to respond to a situation in a positive way rather than react to a situation in a negative way.

Every time you meet someone, there is an exchange of energy. If you are happy and find the meeting was enjoyable, then the energy exchange is neutral.

However, if you lose control of your emotions and become angry, the other person steals your energy.

Likewise, if someone gets angry at you then you are stealing their energy. With this simple philosophy, you can counter the endless situations or people that in the past have triggered your anger and caused you to react in an unhealthy manner.

Next time someone honks their car horn at you or criticises you for no apparent reason, smile and say to yourself I am not going to let you steal my energy.

Just imagine how much better you will feel when you choose not to react to negative people or situations.

How many times in the past have you shouted abuse at another car driver and still felt the anger in your stomach an hour or so later.

That person stole your energy. They probably drove on laughing at how silly you looked when you lost your composure.

You allowed them to cause you stress, anger and probably indigestion. Only one person came out of this confrontation with their energy intact and it wasn't you.

Anger is a choice response. Decide each day not to allow your energy to be stolen from you by negative people or situations. On a physical level, anger can cause stomach and digestive disorders.

Choose to live a healthier life free from anger.

Use Reiki to assist the re-balancing process. Place one hand on the third eye chakra and the other hand on the root chakra. Keep your hands there for as long as you intuitively feel is necessary.

This Reiki technique will help you control and eliminate this destructive emotion.

It can be used for self healing or on another person.

Just For Today I Will Not Worry

Worry causes stress and anxiety leading to an imbalance of the mind, body, and spirit and blockage to the root chakra.

The best way to overcome worry is to accept that all of us are faced with difficulties and setbacks in our lives.

How we respond to them determines how we ultimately lead our lives.

If you choose to respond negatively by getting upset and anxious towards one of life's setbacks, you have chosen to damage the balance of your mind body and spirit.

If you respond positively by accepting the setback as an opportunity to learn, you can live a happier and more fulfilling life.

Allow yourself time each day to really laugh and have fun.

Watch a funny movie or television show. Read a humorous book or magazine.

Whatever it takes to make you laugh, do it. Ralph Waldo Emerson said, "Man surrounds himself with images of himself." This wonderful pearl of wisdom teaches us that if you want to be happy, mix with happy people.

Likewise, if you want to be negative and constantly worrying, you simply need to associate with people who are negative and worrisome. Laughter is a wonderful healer.

It has been proven through numerous studies that laughter can heal and in some cases prevent life threatening illnesses.

Use this knowledge to live a healthier and longer life. Take responsibility for how you deal with life's setbacks. Have fun life's too short to waste it by in worry.

Use Reiki to re-balance your mind, body, and spirit and boost your resolve. Place one hand on the root chakra and the other hand on the heart chakra.

Reiki will bring your mind body and spirit into equilibrium.

Keep your hands over these chakra points for as long as you intuitively feel you need to.

This Reiki technique will remove the blockages caused by stress, worry and anxiety. It can be used for self healing or on another person.

Just For Today I Will Be Humble

Life tends to give us what we need, it may not be what we want but it will be what we need.

Throughout our lives, we receive what we need to grow and learn in this lifetime. If we grasp these lessons and grow accordingly, we will become spiritually enlightened.

Instead of wasting your life complaining of the things that have happened to you, and the problems you face.

Step back for a moment on a regular basis, discover and appreciate the many blessings in your life.

Make a list of all your blessings. You will be amazed at how many wonderful things there are to give thanks for. Leave the materialistic things aside.

They are shallow and meaningless.

Pay attention to, and focus on the things that are free and bring joy and humility to your life.

For example, your mind, body, spirit, health, family, friends, flowers, trees, sea, sun, love, faith, knowledge, the countryside, animals, birds, etc., the list is endless.

When you appreciate the true wonders of life and let go of the materialistic things you are bound to enjoy your life more.

Place one hand on the third eye chakra and the other hand on the occipital ridge.

Use Reiki to re-balance this principle in your life or in the life of another person.

Just For Today I Will Do My Work Honestly

Honesty means different things to different people.

Many people feel it is fine to take home a few pens from the office, the company turns over millions in profit each year so they can afford to lose a few items of stationery.

While another person will judge the same incident as an act of theft and believe that anyone found stealing stationery should be dismissed and charged with theft and even prosecuted.

Everyone at some point is dishonest. You may not steal from another person or company, but instead steal from yourself.

For example, if you a have a talent to help people and you choose not to, then you are stealing from yourself by denying your gift.

You are also stealing from the people who could benefit from your talents.

Wasting your time on meaningless pursuits such as watching television for hours each day is stealing from your sacred and special time on Earth.

Try to live your life to the best of your ability as honestly as you can.

Honesty lives inside of you and doesn't care about being placed where others can view it.

Be Compassionate to Yourself and Other

The law of karma states that what goes around comes around.

Send out love and you will receive love back in return.

Send out kindness and you will receive kindness.

Send out healing and you receive healing.

Send out positive thoughts and you will receive positive results.

Karma is a two edge sword.

Send out negative thoughts and you will get negative results.

Living within this precept will give you a happier and less stressful life, full of joy, peace and love.

To bring balance to this principle for yourself or others, first, place one hand on the third eye chakra and the other hand on the root chakra.

When you feel you are ready, move your hand from the third eye chakra to the throat chakra, and move your hand from the root chakra to the heart chakra keeping it there until you intuitively feel you have finished.

It is important to remember that the Reiki principles are only guides for a happier and more fulfilling life. Use meditation to unlock the true meaning of these precepts and incorporate them into your life. They will transform your life.

Reiki Basic System

• **It Consists of 3 levels, namely ;**

Reiki 1 (Practitioners start to connect with Reiki)
Reiki 2 (The right to use Three Reiki Symbols)
Reiki Master (The Right to provide of attunement to others)

Necessitate Self Healing for 21 days*

* it requires self-healing for 21 days
* It is Considered as the first Western tradition of reiki and a recommended basis for those who want to start studying Reiki.

Attunements

The ability to channel divine energy should be attained through attunements. Without an attunement, you can channel energy, but the energy you channel is regular energy from your surroundings, normally called prana.

Why is an attunement so important? How is it possible that even the level 1 attunement can give us the ability to channel divine energy?
Let us examine the details of the attunement and what is done to your energy body that gives you the ability to channel energy simply by having the intention.

First, it is important to understand that a Reiki attunement is not an energy transfer. The Master giving the attunement does not give you energy.
The Master channels energy to cleanse and open your energy channels and the chakras that connect you to divine energy and the earth's core energy.

As you become better connected to the unlimited divine energy and the earth's core energy, your energy centers or chakras will open.

Some of the divine energy and earth's core energy will flow automatically toward you even though you haven't started any energy channeling. This is the reason why you feel an increased level of energy right after the attunement, even though you have not done any exercises yet.

Indeed, if you let the energy flow through you by doing energy channeling, some of the energy will be left within you.
The more you channel energy, the more energy you will receive and the quality of your energy will also improve.

You should get an attunement initiation first, before practicing further Reiki.

The attunement initiation process can be obtained through the nearest Reiki master in your city.
In this era of googling it is very easy to find that information.
Make sure your Reiki lineage is officially accredited

Reiki Tradition

- *Vajra Reiki*
- *Rainbow Reiki*
- *Usui-Tibetan Reiki*
- *Tera-Mai Reiki*
- *Seichim Reiki*
- *Tummo Reiki*
- *Prema Reiki*
- *Golden Reiki*

New Reiki Tradition

- *Sacred Path Reiki*
- *Quantum Reiki*
- *Tibetan Soul Star Reiki*
- *Tibetan Reiki*
- *Radiant Technique Reiki*
- *Neo Zen Reiki*
- *Karuna Reiki*
- *Raku Kai Reiki*
- *Johrei Reiki*

Etc.

Advantages of REIKI

We have discussed the benefits of REIKI for your health and spiritual growth. Now let us look at some of its advantages ;

Easy to Learn

Learning REIKI is easy and simple. You don't need a special background or knowledge to learn Reiki and you can learn the basic techniques in several hours.
 You don't have to memorize anything and when you leave the workshop after a few hours, you can start using Reiki because you are already a channel and can channel energy to yourself and to others.

 You will have also practiced different energy channeling techniques during the workshop., either by yourself or in a group. As a channel, you connect yourself to an unlimited source of energy. You are indeed connected to the Creator. It is this easy to learn REIKI.

Easy to Practice

Reiki is easy to practice. The most important practice consists of channeling energy to yourself to make you, the practitioner, more relaxed, more refreshed, and healthier each day.
You can channel energy simply by placing your palms directly on the body part you want to channel the energy to, or even to objects.

Although you would obtain the best results if you practice in an ideal environment, you can also achieve good results by practicing anywhere and at different times. You can channel energy when waiting at the bus stop, airport, railway station, or other places.

You can also channel energy during meetings, when driving a car, talking on the phone, watching TV or during other activities. Imagine how easy it is for you to practice Reiki.

Even without practice, the two energies in REIKI, the divine energy and the Kundalini energy, will continue to work without interruption.

You can channel energy while you are talking, writing, walking, smiling, even when you are doing nothing.

As for Kundalini energy, as long as your body posture is good, the Kundalini works 24 hours a day to cleanse your energy body and increase your energy vibration.

Even though you are aware that these two extraordinary energies will continue to work automatically, do not be lazy. Without practice, your advancement will be very slow.

Only with routine practice can you obtain the greatest benefits from REIKI.

Channeling/Healing Is Easy

In channeling energy with REIKI, you don't have to be concerned with how to access the energy. All you need to do is simply to have the intention to channel energy. You only need to do this once.

That is all. Once you intend to channel energy, you can channel energy as long as you want.

In channeling the energy, not all of the energy you access flows out of your body. Some of the energy stays within you.

The energy that is flowing through you is actually cleansing your energy channels and increasing your energy.

So, although your energy has already improved in terms of quantity and quality with the attunement, the more you channel, the more the quantity and quality of your energy will improve.

When you do a healing session, you don't need to worry about diagnosing, finding negative energy, removing negative energy, when to stop channeling, and so forth.

In fact, you don't even have to think about any of this. All you need to do is simply lay your hands on your body or the body of someone else.

The intelligent divine energy flowing from your palms does all the work, such as locating and removing negative energy and pumping in clean energy.

The energy stops flowing when it is no longer needed. At the time you are channeling the energy, you can feel that you are more relaxed. So, when you channel energy, all you need to do is smile, relax and enjoy.

Channeling/Healing Is Safe

It is important to know that channeling/healing with REIKI is safe and you and your client will not contaminate each another.
You know that you are not pure, that there are still impurities within you and your energy channel. As the energy flows through you and through your energy channel, the energy brings some of your impurities out together with the energy.

Therefore, while you are channeling energy to a client, Some of the negativities and impurities from your energy channel are passed on to your client's body because it was removed from your own body during the process.

Fortunately, the percentage of negativity coming from your body and into your client is normally very little compared to the clean energy being channeled. Thus, in most cases, this is insignificant.
With Reiki, occurrences like these rarely happen. The divine energy you channel is intelligent enough to be able to separate the negative energy from your own body from the divine energy itself.

So, only divine energy flows into your clients when you are channeling energy to them. Also, when you channel energy to yourself, only clean energy will flow from your palms.

There is another matter that is important in energy channeling. When you channel other types of energy to a client, the clean energy pushes out negativity and impurities from your client.
Some of the impurities may flow towards you and contaminate you.
In contrast, when you channel energy with Reiki, the divine energy flows continuously from your palms.

At the same time, some of the energy also flows out from your whole body, building a stronger aura around you and protecting you from the negativity that is released by your client.

So you can see how safe it is to channel Reiki, It is safe for both you, as the channel, and for your client as the recipient of the energy.

Benefits of REIKI

The practice of Reiki can affect every element of a person's life from the physical, emotional and mental aspects to the spiritual dimensions. As a Reiki practitioner, you can expect the following benefits:

- Reiki will relax you when you are stressed
- Reiki brings about deep relaxation
- Reiki centres your thoughts when you are confused
- Reiki energises you when you feel drained
- Reiki calms you when you are frightened
- Reiki focuses your mind and helps you to solve problems
- Reiki relieves pain
- Reiki accelerates natural healing of wounds
- Reiki improves health
- Reiki gradually heals chronic diseases
- Reiki helps preventing the development of disease
- Reiki detoxifies the body
- Reiki dissolves energy blockages
- Reiki releases emotional wounds
- Reiki increases the vibrational frequency of the body
- Reiki helps changing negative conditioning & behavior
- Better connection with the Divine
- Improving and maintaining your health
- Healing physical, mental, and emotional problems
- Cleansing the energy body
- Increasing the quantity and quality of your energy
- Protection
- Enhanced relaxation
- Support for meditation
- Improvement of other energy works
- Smoother skin
- Awakening the Kundalini and assisting the cleansing/purifying process of the Kundalini
- Elevating awareness

Better Connection with the Divine

Technically speaking, the connection to the Divine is the connection between the crown chakra and the Divine chakra. It is called **antakarana**.

A wider antakarana generates a better connection to the Divine.
The thickness or size of the antakarana reflects the degree of opening of the crown chakra.
Unfortunately, the antakarana of most people is as thick as a hair.

This gives us an idea of how narrow the opening of the crown chakra is in most people.
After a Reiki attunement, the crown chakra is opened much wider and this directly influences the size of your antakarana.

If you are sensitive, you can actually feel that your connection to the Divine has improved. When you pray, you can feel more Divine blessing flowing into your heart and your whole being.

This, of course, will have an impact on your everyday life.

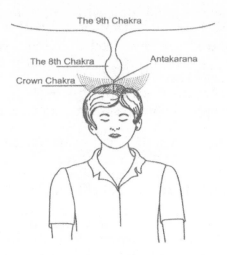

The antakarana in most people is as thick as a hair.

The antakarana of a level 2 Reiki practitioner

You should understand that when your antakarana becomes thicker, it does not mean that you will automatically become holier.

The antakarana simply facilitates your connection to Divine Source.

Whether you make good use of this facility or not is entirely up to you. Having a thicker antakarana is like having a larger pipe installed.
You still need to open the tap to make use of the larger pipe. The tap is your heart.
You need to open your heart before the Divine blessing can flow through your antakarana into your heart and into your whole being.

Improving and Maintaining Health

The Reiki attunement gives you an instant ability to channel energy and as in other Reiki traditions, you are able to channel energy to improve your health.
 If you practice regularly, all negative energy inside your body will be pushed out and the energy surrounding your body will thicken, providing you with better protection.

Many of our alumni have realized this benefit. Some alumni who were not in good health before their attunement and had frequent colds, for example, or got sick easily, experienced improved health after their attunement.
 I have received many letters from happy alumni explaining that their health improved dramatically after Reiki attunements and many have stayed healthy afterwards.

 This benefit is not only for the Reiki practitioner, but also for those who regularly receive energy channeling treatments from a practitioner.
Although the chance to help others is a blessing, not all or you can afford the time to do so. In learning Reiki, it is not necessary to become a healer. You simply use the technique to channel energy to yourself so you can become healthier.

There is one thing you have to remember. Being a Reiki practitioner does not make you a super man or woman. You still need to take care of your health by eating healthy food, getting enough rest, and exercising regularly.
 Once you have taken care of these basic physical needs, then by practicing Reiki regularly you can expect to enjoy improved health.

Healing Physical, Mental, and Emotional Problems

For those who have health problems, the divine energy from Reiki is a positive healing force. The divine energy works well in healing physical, mental, and emotional problems.
Most types of clean energy can be used to heal physical illnesses.
although some may be better then others. Coarser energies tend to not be suitable for healing mental or emotional problems because the problems are not located in the physical body, but in the mental and emotional body layers .
Energies with coarser particles can only reach the physical body layer and are unable to extend to the higher or finer body layers.

The mental and emotional body layers are at a higher level than the physical body layer. On the other hand, the finer particles of divine energy in Reiki can reach all body layers without difficulty. So the divine energy in Reiki can heal mental and emotional problems as well as physical ones

For those who are experiencing stress and sleeping difficulties, learning Reiki will relieve you from your mental and emotional problems within a few days. You will be able to have a better quality of sleep more easily. A gentleman once enrolled in our workshops for Reiki levels 1 and 2 (held consecutively for two days).

He attended the first level workshop on a Saturday, but failed to show up on Sunday for the level 2workshop. On Monday he called to tell us that he overslept and could not arrive on time for the second workshop session.

In fact, he said, he had been suffering from sleeping difficulties for almost seven years. Usually he would fall sleep at dawn and only for a few hours. But after the Reiki workshop on Saturday night, he went straight to bed and slept until11AM on Sunday.
He came to the next workshop several months later and told us that his sleeping problems were over. Not only could he sleep more easily, he said, but the quality of his sleep was much better.

Cleansing the Energy Body

If you are serious about your spiritual growth, one of the most important first steps you should take is cleansing your energy body. In channeling energy with Reiki, you take this crucial step as the divine energy cleanses your physical, mental, and emotional body layers. So, even if you do not have any physical, mental or emotional problems, energy channeling provides you with essential benefits.

If you are a REIKI practitioner, your energy body is being cleansed continuously 24 hours a day. You are connected both to the divine and earth core energies and while the divine energy works on you directly, the earth core energy flows into your perineum, activating and uncoiling your Kundalini energy.

This enables your Kundalini energy to cleanse you simultaneously. Divine energy and Kundalini energy work in synergy giving you the best results. However, to ensure that both energies work at their best continuously, you must be aware of two factors:

You need to open your heart to allow the divine energy to flow in and you need to maintain correct body posture to let the Kundalini energy flow properly along your sushumna.

Increasing the Quantity and Quality of Your Energy

No matter what your background is, no matter what energy work you have done before whether in one of the Reiki traditions or another energy work system right after the Reiki level 1 attunement, the quality and quantity of your energy will increase significantly.

The increase in energy means, among other things, that you are more fit and energized in your everyday life and that you can channel energy more effectively.

Protection

The energy surrounding your body creates a protective energy layer called the aura. The thicker this protective energy layer is, the more difficult it is for negative energy and disease to penetrate the body. After receiving a Reiki attunement, your aura becomes much thicker and has better quality.

Since the energy that is protecting you is a special blessing from the Divine Source, the energy is intelligent beyond human comprehension and can help you in many ways without you even telling it what to do.

For example, it there is a negative presence around you, your aura will immediately thicken much more providing you with better protection. As a practitioner, you also learn a technique to help protect others who are non-practitioners.

Enhanced Relaxation

As expressed earlier, divine energy can cleanse mental and emotional body layers where stress usually accumulates.
When channeling energy either to yourself or to others, you allow the divine energy and Kundalini energy to flow and work on you while they are flowing through you. Both energies cleanse your mental and emotional body layers helping you to be calmer and more relaxed.

Being calm and relaxed is invaluable. Most of us do not realize it, but we experience an enormous amount of stress in our daily lives. This statement is not limited to adults.
Children can experience stress as well.
You may have noticed that when you tell your children to study, they suddenly become hungry, thirsty or need to go to the bathroom. Children who behave like this are usually not just making up excuses, they are experiencing stress.

We all desire peace and calmness in our lives. We do not want to be anxious, tense or in states of unease.
Unfortunately, our surroundings and the conditions of our everyday lives inflict a lot of stress on us. Noise, pollution, family situations, the demands of our jobs, hectic schedules, and many other circumstances of modern life are constant creators of stress. Most of the time, it is difficult to free ourselves from these stressors.

Fortunately, as a Reiki practitioner you can do away with stress easily by channeling energy. Once you are free from stress, you can regain higher quality of life.

Support for Meditation

There are hundreds of meditation techniques. Most basic techniques help you to be more relaxed and healthier.

The more advanced techniques practiced by serious spiritual seekers involve the attainment of the Divine blessing.

As a Reiki practitioner, you are more relaxed so you can achieve a meditative state with ease. Since the gate to the Divine blessing your crown chakra is already open, you can receive the Divine blessing much more easily. The result of this is that the quality of your meditation will improve tremendously.

You will be able to quickly obtain a higher quality of meditative state in a relatively short period of time. In fact, when your heart opens wide enough you will be able to receive so much of the blessings that you will be able to experience complete bliss.
 At the same time, your connection to the earth energy keeps you grounded. So, you can experience and enjoy the bliss while still functioning in your daily life.
There is an interesting fact related to meditation and Reiki.

Usually, when you are meditating you attract the presence of many non-physical beings since you are accumulating a great deal of energy. The beings will want to obtain some of the energy too. Some of them may actually sap your energy.
The situation is completely different when you meditate from the heart after receiving the Reiki attunement. When you meditate from the heart, your special connection to the Divine makes your whole being glow in light and non-physical beings are unable to get close to you.

Also, it is impossible for other beings to take energy from you.

Improvement of Other Energy Work

As already stated, different methods of energy work may involve different types of energy. Yet most of the energy has to flow through the same energy channel in the body, the sushumna, which is the main energy channel within the spine. Though a practitioner of another energy work will normally require years of serious practice to open the sushumna all the way from the base chakra to the crown chakra, with Reiki,the whole sushumna is opened instantly at the very first level.

Once the whole sushumna is open, you can allow other energies to flow through your sushumna at will. As your whole being starts to become cleaner, your chakras will also be cleaner. Thus, any other energy work you may do will improve. You can absorb and direct the flow of energies easily, even the "chi" type of energy that is used in the martial arts.

Smoother Skin

Channeling energy in Reiki helps the regeneration of body cells.
Therefore, if you channel the energy every day for one or two weeks, you will find that your skin becomes smoother. Not only does your complexion improve, but other common skin problems, such as acne, will also improve with time.

As a result of improved health conditions and smoother skin, those who practice REIKI usually look younger than their age.

Awakening the Kundalini and Assisting the Cleansing/Purifying Process of the Kundalini

If you are serious about spiritual growth, whether you are still searching or already on the path, you have probably heard about Kundalini.

You know that many people who practice different traditions of yoga are trying to awaken their Kundalini because of its critical role in the attainment of Yoga, the Oneness.
Unfortunately, the Kundalini is very difficult to awaken. You need to practice special techniques to awaken the Kundalini and it still takes decades of serious and dedicated practice before your Kundalini awakens.

The problem with Kundalini awakening does not end there. Even after your Kundalini is awakened, you still have to take special care to prevent difficulties caused by your Kundalini awakening, the so-called Kundalini syndrome.

In Reiki , there is no Kundalini syndrome. Your Kundalini is awakened instantly on the second level attunement and it will be a safe awakening. Our tens of thousands of alumni can attest to this fact.

Our alumni have all had their Kundalini awakened and they have experienced significant improvement in their general conditions compared to the time before they learned Reiki.

 Reiki attunements have also offered a solution to those who are performing Kundalini practice using traditional methods and have had problems for years.

Remember, the difficulty with Kundalini awakening is that in traditional methods, the Kundalini is awakened while the sushumna has not yet opened.

So, there is no passage for the energy to flow through. An awakened Kundalini has a strong energy that creates pressure if it is blocked and has nowhere to go. That is when the Kundalini energy pushes against different parts of the body and creates problems.

However, as already mentioned, in the REIKI attunement, your whole sushumna is opened thoroughly during the first level attunement as preparation for your Kundalini awakening.
The second level attunement opens your sushumna even wider. As your Kundalini awakens, the unobstructed energy passage is there, ready to be used by Kundalini energy.

The uncoiled Kundalini energy can then flow easily along your sushumna and burst out from your crown chakra giving you bliss, not pain. For those who are familiar with Kundalini awakening, it is a near miracle to be able to have it safely awakened in one quick attunement.

With your Kundalini awakening, the critical cleansing of your whole being begins.

Working in synergy with the divine energy, your Kundalini works so fast and efficiently that you can expect to get the core of your Kundalini into your crown chakra in only a few years.

This is a significant accomplishment since most people consider that the Kundalini process normally takes more than a lifetime.

Elevating Awareness

After the REIKI attunement, you may notice that your awareness has changed and your negative reactions to various situations have been substantially reduced. From a spiritual point of view, energy channeling capability is not the most important accomplishment.

The most important technique and training is LIFE. Yes, your daily life and how you face it are the most important exercises in spirituality.

True spirituality is not about Supernatural powers or skills. True spirituality is a journey into the heart to realize the truth and to come closer to the Creator so as to attain Yoga.

In a relatively short period of time, your awareness will increase, giving ou exceptional benefits for your daily life and for your spiritual advancement.

 The benefits associated with a higher level of awareness will undoubtedly increase the quality of your life. It can mean avoiding potential problems because you will not have overlooked small but significant details.

It can mean avoiding a potential hazard because you decided to take one course of action over another, even though it may seem more logical to go with the worse one.
We have all had experiences when we felt we should do something but did not, only to end up in some sort of mess, regretting not following what we "felt" we should have done.

Increased awareness is priceless in our daily lives and can play a major role in preventing us from encountering many pitfalls. It can pave the way for a less stressful and more peaceful life.

Basic Exercises

- **Basic Technique of Energy Channeling**

Feel the Reiki phenomenon! Relax, sincere, do not push yourself, and do not concentrate

- **Training of palms sensitivity**

Feel the Reiki vibration phenomenon flowing through the palms chakras.

- **Reiki Mawashi**
Feel the flow of Reiki energy channeled by others!

- **Channeling Reiki Into Drinking Water**
Simple trial to channel Reiki at a distance

Reiki practitioners have the ability to utilize Reiki for self-healing or healing to others.

Ethics in Healing

There are several ethical considerations that you, as a Reiki practitioner, should note.

• Healing should be done with the client's permission
• Never take advantage of a client
• Never use energy channeling for your own benefit
• If you receive payment, never ignore poor people
• Never diagnose a client's illness
• Never promise a cure

Healing Should Be Done with the Client's Permission

In healing with Reiki , you may channel the energy or heal only if you have obtained permission from the client or the client's family. You should not send energy to a client who refuses to receive a healing.

Never Take Advantage of a Client

it is better to channel energy by placing your hands directly on the client's body .
But, ask for your client's permission before you start. if your client does not like to be touched at specific parts of the body or does not like to be touched at all, don't do so.

When you channel energy to a client of the opposite sex, you should place your hands only where it is more appropriate.

Never Use Energy Channeling for Your Own Benefit

In healing, an energy exchange is beneficial and will provide better results for the client.
Thus, it is acceptable to receive payment from a client for whom you channeled healing.
 Therefore, please limit the payment to a reasonable professional fee only

If You Receive Payment, Never Ignore the Poor

Although an energy exchange helps the client to be more open for healing,
you still have to consider poor clients.
Keep in mind that all energy is from the Creator and you are only a mediator.
If you have a fixed fee for your services, you should give special consideration to poor clients.

Never Diagnose a Client's Illness

Please remember that learning about energy in REIKI is simply a tool to understanding more about the heart and the divine blessing.

This helps you to be within your heart so that the divine blessing can work at its best on and through you.

 You are still limited by human constraints. So rather than learning to become a good healer, you will learn to become a better channel by allowing the divine blessing to work more.

Channeling energy for healing is simply the introductory step to being able to surrender better to the divine blessing.
You want to allow the divine blessing to help you on so many other matters as you progress to more advanced levels.
This is about letting the divine blessing work on you and through you.

 Therefore, you don't want to diagnose illness. You are not in the position nor have the authority to do so.
It is also not recommended to do non-physical checkups on your client.

Technically speaking, those of you who know more about energy and its relation with health know that the energy body is much more sensitive than the physical body, In many cases, an illness usually emerges first on the energy body and then on the physical body.

While a medical checkup may not show any problem with a particular organ of the body, the problem can be detected at non physical level already.

Thus, you can actually recognize the problems before it actually manifests in the physical body. However, one important thing to note is that you do not have the legal qualifications to give a diagnosis. Thus, you should not give a diagnosis to your client.

Of course, if you see that the client's kidney is unclean you may give suggestions such as "drink more water" and the like.
But, never give a diagnosis such as "your kidney is not well", because formally your diagnosis cannot be proven. If the client goes to see a medical doctor to check her/his kidney later and no problem is found at all, your client may draw negative conclusions.

Never Promise a Cure

When you channel Reiki correctly, your client will surely benefit.
However, the benefit obtained may not necessarily be a cure.

Complete recovery comes from the Creator's blessing and permission. Thus, never promise a cure to your clients.

Frequently Asked Questions and Answers

• My father is very skeptical about non-physical matters like energy channeling. He has rheumatism and I want to try to heal him with Reiki energy. But, if I ask his permission, I am sure he will refuse.
What is the best thing I can do?

Theoretically, if you want to channel energy to someone you should have the person's permission first. But in practice, many agree that if your intention is good and wholly to help the client, then you can send energy to the client in need without the client's permission.
For people who are skeptical about energy work, sometimes it is better to channel energy without asking for permission first. If you have already offered and the person has refused, a protective shell will form that will not allow the energy that you channel to penetrate. You should note that the result will not be as good as for clients who are cooperative.

• I have been a healer for many years and I am clairvoyant. If I see that a client's organ has problems, shall I just keep this to myself?

You can give suggestions to help your client handle the problem and at the same time suggest that your client see a medical doctor. Never give a diagnosis, such as, saying that an organ is ill or that an organ is not functioning well.

Other Techniques

After learning the basics of energy channeling/healing with Reiki and learning the important principles, let us look at other techniques that can be performed by a level 1 Reiki practitioner

Distant Energy Channeling

Even if you are only a level 1 practitioner, you can do energy channeling remotely.

However, normally, the recipient who is located at a distance from your location will not receive 100% of your energy.
You can compensate for this problem easily by channeling the energy longer
.
Generally, a practitioner at a higher level can channel energy distantly better. As a level I REIKI practitioner, if you practice regularly your capability will increase gradually.

With Reiki , distant energy channeling can be done easily. With some other energy work, you need much information about the recipient
.
Sometimes a photograph is required in order to channel energy to that person. But to channel Reiki energy at a distance you only need to use a loose reference to the person to whom you will channel the energy.

 For example:
• Jack Smith who lives in California or
• Ashley Dunn's cousin or
• The client introduced by Mr. Paul (you forgot the name)

With only references such as these, you can start distant energy channeling.
Before you start channeling, you need an object to act as a "replacement target" for the client.

The following replacement targets are often used in distant healing:
1, An object as a model or replacement for the client (for example, adoll or a teddy bear).

2. Part of your body. For example, one of your thighs, where your knee is considered as the client's head. Although in general, Reiki healing does not contaminate the client or the healer, the use of your own body as a replacement target is an exception.
Therefore, it is not recommended to use a part of your own body as a replacement target to channel energy distantly.
When using your own body, there is a risk that some of the negative energy from your client can contaminate you. By using your own body as a target, you unite your non-physical body layer with your client's allowing the negative energy from your client to enter easily into your own energy body.

3. Imagine that your client is present in front of you, without the use of any physical replacement object. You can imagine the client as standing, sitting, or lying down. The client's size is not necessarily the same as the real size.

The method for distant energy channeling is exactly the same as when a client is present in front of you. You can channel energy locally or to the whole body.

You can use any object as a replacement target: a piece of paper, a book, a doll, a table, and so on. A doll is preferable because it makes it easier for you to know which part of the client's body you are channeling energy to.
If you use a piece of paper, after you channel energy for some time in a very relaxed condition, you might lose count of the body positions.
The same principles apply in both direct healing and distant healing.

The relaxed condition of the client during energy channeling is important to obtain better results.
It is best to agree with the client on a convenient time to send the energy. That way, the client can prepare and relax to receive the energy.

If you do not fix a time with the client, and you are unable to call the client, then you can send the energy when you think that the client is sleeping.

After you learn level 2, you can ensure that the client will receive the energy when they are relaxed since you can direct the energy to reach the client at any time you want. For example, you can direct the energy to reach the client at a time when the client is asleep.

Chakra Balancing

A chakra is an energy center and also the center of emotions. The higher chakras in your body are more spiritually orientated. The lower chakras will draw you to worldly matters.

Imbalanced chakras will cause you to become either too spiritual or too worldly.
With the Reiki attunement, the whole length of your sushumna is opened so energy can flow equally to all the chakras.

Thus, excess energy in one chakra can be easily distributed to other chakras automatically. But, it is still advisable for you to balance your chakras occasionally Chakra balancing is easy. Basically, you only channel energy to the two chakras that have opposite qualities at the same time.

For example, if your right hand channels energy to your crown chakra, your left hand channels energy to your base chakra at the same time.

There is no requirement on which hand to use for a specific chakra, as long as you channel energy to two opposite chakras at the same time according to the following sequence:

- Base chakra- Crown chakra
- Sacral chakra- Throat chakra
- Navel chakra- Heart chakra
- Ajna chakra- Front and back

The first balancing is between the base and the crown chakras. The base chakra, the center of physical matters and the foundation of your worldly life, should be balanced with the crown chakra, the center for your spiritual life.

Next, the sacral chakra, the center of lower creation, should be balanced with the throat chakra, the center of creativity (higher creation) and communication. The navel chakra, the ego center, is balanced with the heart chakra, the center of attention for others.

Finally, the front and back of the ajna chakra are balanced because the ajna chakra is the center of the mind and the soul.

Reducing Stress

If you or your clients are often stressed, energy channeling at the following positions will help reduce stress.
The energy channeling below is similar to chakra balancing, except the sets of chakras are different. Of course, whole body energy channeling is still important, so this is a technique that should supplement the whole body treatment.
- Ajna chakra- Front and back
- Navel Chakra- Heart chakra
- Solar plexus chakra- Heart chakra

The solar plexus chakra has been added in this technique. The solar plexus chakra is the center of ambition. Someone whose solar plexus chakra is overly active may do negative things to others in order to gain personal benefits.

The solar plexus chakra has to be balanced with the heart chakra, the center of love and compassion. Many people who experience high levels of stress have problems with the solar plexus chakra because it is either overly active or blocked.

Chakra balancing as described above, in addition to a full body energy channeling, will speed up the healing.

Additional Channeling

The best results can be obtained if you take extra time to be relaxed, smiling and surrendering when you channel energy.

Energy channeling with Reiki in this condition allows you to not only heal and cleanse yourself, but to also let the divine blessing of the Reiki energy work on your heart to make it stronger.

When you do this after you are level 2 or higher, the energy channeling itself will automatically cleanse, open and strengthen your heart at the same time that you channel energy to your whole body.

You can also channel energy when you are doing other activities and the result will be quite satisfactory.
Ask yourself:
• Do you drive?
• Do you wait at bus stops, railway stations, or airports?
• Do you attend meetings?
• Do you watch television or go to the movies?

Whenever you engage in routine activities that do not require you to move your hands or in which you are not disturbed, you can channel energy.

To channel the energy, it is only necessary to have the initial intention. Here are the steps to take:
1. Shake your hands two or three times.

2. Have the intention to channel REIKI and feel the energy flowing from your palms and fingertips.

3. Place your hands on your lap, on the table, on your suitcase, or on the steering wheel, while saying in your heart to whom you want to channel the energy (it can be to yourself) and to which part of the body.
As long as you do not move your hands, the energy will keep flowing. If you move your hands, you need to repeat the procedure
from step 1.

4. As Soon as you position your hands, your attention can be directed to other matters. There is no need to keep your attention on channeling since the energy will continue to flow without difficulty.

You can also do this method before you go to sleep. Before falling asleep, have the intention to channel energy to one part of your body or to your whole body and then place your hands so as not to disturb your sleep. Channeling energy before falling asleep can help you sleep easier and better.

Channeling Energy into Drinking Water and Food

Reiki energy can be channeled not only into your body, but also into your drinking water, food, and medicines. You can channel energy into drinking water and give it to your client to drink after a healing session.

The combination of the energy channeled directly into the body and the energy in the drinking water will give better results.

Channeling energy into drinking water or food is easy.

Just intend to channel Reiki energy and direct your hands to the glass of water or to your food.

Channeling energy into drinking water (or food)

Balancing the Yin and the Yang

We know that the energy inside our body has two different characteristics: they are yin (cold) and yang (hot). If the yin and yang in the body are balanced a person tends to be healthy.

You can balance the yin and yang easily by doing the following steps:

I. Shake your hands two or three times.

2. Relax and smile.

3. Have the intention to channel REIKI energy and wait until you feel the energy flowing from your palms and fingertips.

4. Now, put your palms together with the intention that the energy from your left hand will flow to the whole right side of your body, and the energy from your right hand to the left side of your body.

5. Relax and let the energy work for 5-10 minutes.

Balancing the Yin and Yang

Reiki Meditation

Most meditation techniques are not really meditation techniques. They are only relaxation techniques. Scientifically, how deeply someone is doing a meditation can be measured by that person's brain waves.

A person who is simply in a relaxed condition has a brain wave of between 8 and 12 Hz, often called the alpha state. A person entering a meditation state has a brain wave of between 4 and7 Hz, often called the theta state. With Reiki , you can do a simple meditation that not only cleanses your body, but also brings you into the theta state or true meditation.

The method is easy. After you find a quiet place where you will not be disturbed, do the following:
1. Shake your hands two or three times.
2. Relax and smile.
3. Have the intention to channel REIKI energy and wait until you feel the energy flowing from your palms and fingertips.
4. Place your hands face down on your lap with your palms touching your lap, Have the intention that the energy from your left palm flows to the whole left side of your body and the energy from your right palm flows to the whole right side of your body
5. Close your eyes and direct your attention to your heart chakra,

Grounding Technique

Since this technique is so beneficial not only for you as a Reiki practitioner, but also for the public, feel free to share it with others.

However, bear in mind that there is an important difference for Reiki practitioners when doing the grounding technique.

After receiving Reiki attunement, you are connected better to your heart. For this reason, you do not want to use visualization to imagine the flow of the energy.

All you need to do is simply have the intention. The energy will flow according to your intention.

If you have the "Grounding Technique" cassette or CD, you only need to listen to it and the energy will flow as intended.

Figure 31a

Figure 31b

Figure 31c

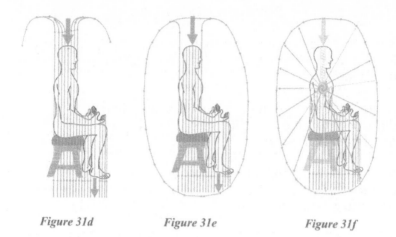

Figure 31d   Figure 31e   Figure 31f

Figure 31a: Divine energy fills and cleanses the chakras and the body.

Figure 31b: Divine energy flows down to the center of the Earth.

Figure 31c: The Earth's core energy starts rising.

Figure 31d: The Earth's core energy rises through the body and above the crown chakra. It forms the upper part of a giant energy ball while Divine energy still flows down through the crown chakra to the center of the Earth.

Figure 31e: The giant energy ball is formed.

Figure 31f Divine energy and the Earth's energy mix at the heart chakra and spread to all parts of the body and around the body, filling the giant energy ball.

• Locate a quiet room where you will not be disturbed during practice. Dim the light so that you can be more relaxed.

 If possible, you can play music with nature sounds such as running water or you can play New Age music. You can also burn incense or use essential oils made especially for assisting relaxation.

• Sit down and relax either on a chair or on the floor (with a rug or mat).

• Make sure your spine is straight without forcing yourself. If you sit on a chair, try not to lean on it. If this is difficult, you may lean on the chair, as long as your back is straight.
• Close your eyes so that you can focus your attention easier.
• Place your hands on your lap palms-up in a receiving position.
• Inhale deeply without forcing yourself. Exhale and feel that all the tension in your body is breathed out with your exhalation.
• Inhale deeply without forcing yourself. Exhale and feel that your body becomes very relaxed.
• Inhale deeply one more time without forcing yourself. Exhale and feel that your body and mind become very relaxed.
• Now you can start the grounding practice. Focus your attention on your crown chakra. Feel the divine light in the form of bright white light coming down and touching your crown chakra.
 The crown chakra becomes more active, turning to the left and to the right while cleansing itself. More divine light flows to the crown chakra.
The crown chakra becomes cleaner and blossoms like a bright lotus.
• The divine light penetrates the crown chakra at the center and enters the head. It fills up the top, the middle, and then the lower part of the head. From now on, the divine light flows through the crown chakra continuously becoming brighter and stronger with time.
• The divine light will erode all impurities from your head and push them out of the ajna chakra.
• More divine light flows in from above and the light coming out of the ajna chakra becomes cleaner with time. The ajna chakra rotates to the left and to the right, cleansing itself and becoming more active.
Let the light flow for some time until the ajna chakra cleanses even more.

• The divine light flowing into the crown chakra increases, while some of the light still flows from the ajna chakra to expand the ajna chakra further, the rest of the light within the head starts to flow down into the throat.

While flowing into the throat, the light erodes all the impurities and negative energy in the throat and drags them out.

After the throat is full of light, all impurities and negative energies are pushed out through the throat chakra at the center of the throat,

• Let the divine light flow out through the throat chakra until it becomes cleaner with time. The throat chakra rotates to the left and to the right to become cleaner, more active, and more expanded

• The divine light flows down increasingly and starts to enter the top portion of the chest. Some of the divine light enters the left shoulder, the right shoulder, the upper left arm, the upper right arm, the lower left arm, the lower right arm and the fingertips,

The divine light continues to flow, filling up both arms and dragging all impurities from the arms. All tension at the nape of the neck erodes and is dragged out by the divine light.

All the impurities and negative energies are dragged out by the divine light through the right and left palm chakras and the chakras at the fingertips.

• The divine light fills up the upper part of the chest and then flows down to fill the chest up to the diaphragm. All impurities in the cells and body organs in the chest are eroded by the light and dragged out through the heart chakra at the center of the chest,

Let the divine light flow out of the heart chakra and drag out all impurities in the chest.

The chest becomes cleaner with time.

The heart chakra rotates to the left and to the right to become cleaner, more active, and more expanded.

• For those who have problems with their heart, lungs, or respiratory system, imagine the divine light eroding away all the grayish unclean energy in the problem area.

The grayish impure energy is dragged out by the light through the heart chakra and through nearby pores of the skin.

Have the intention to make the particular body part with problems become cleaner and brighter until finally all grayish unclean energy is totally gone and replaced with bright divine light

• The divine light flows through the crown chakra stronger and stronger.

While still flowing out of the ajna chakra, throat chakra, and heart chakra to make all these chakras more developed, some of the divine light starts to flow down through the diaphragm and into the upper abdomen.

The divine light fills up the upper abdomen and cleanses all cells and body organs in the upper abdomen.

The divine light drags out all impurities and negative energy through the navel chakra located at the navel. Let the divine light flow out of the navel chakra dragging out the impurities from the upper abdomen. This area gets cleaner with time. The navel chakra rotates to the left and to the right and becomes cleaner, more active, and more expanded.

• Now, while flowing from the ajna, throat, heart, and navel chakras, the divine light starts to flow down into the lower abdomen.

The divine light fills up the lower abdomen, erodes all impurities and negative energy, and drags them out through the sacral chakra located at the pelvic bone. Let the divine light flow out through the sacral chakra dragging out all the impurities from the lower abdomen. The sacral chakra rotates to the left and to the right to become cleaner, more active and more developed.

• The divine light from the head flows down into the neck bone.

cleansing the neck bone vertebrae by vertebrae while flowing down and dragging all impurities.

The divine light keeps flowing and reaches the spine. The divine light also cleanses the backbone disc by disc until it reaches the tailbone, and also cleanses the tailbone vertebrae by vertebrae.

After reaching the lower end of the tailbone. the divine light flows out through the base chakra located at the end of the tailbone, dragging all the impurities.

Let the divine light flow out through the base chakra until all impurities are totally dragged out.

The base chakra rotates to the left and to the right to become cleaner, more active, and more developed.

• While flowing in through the crown chakra and flowing out through the other six major chakras, the divine light also flows toward the hips, filling the hips.

It then flows and fills the thighs, cleansing as it flows. The divine light then flows toward the knees, ankles and heels, cleansing these body parts as well.

The divine energy finally flows out through the chakras at the arches of the feet and the smaller chakras at the tips of the toes, dragging all impurities out.

• Relax and feel how clean and bright your body is now. The divine light flows continuously through the crown chakra to cleanse the whole body and all the major chakras.

At the same time, divine light flows out through the major chakras, and through the palm chakras, the fingertip chakras, and through the chakras at the arches of the feet and the tips of the toes cleansing your major chakras and your whole body.

If you have health problems, focus your attention on the body part with problems.

Have the intention that all gray energy in the body part is eroded and cleansed by the divine light, and dragged out through nearby pores of the skin.

The body portion with problems becomes cleaner and brighter with time. Feel the body portion becoming clean and healthy.

• Now, if you are sitting on the floor, allow the divine light to flow out through your base chakra to flow down towards the core of the earth.

If you are sitting on a chair with your feet on the floor, let the divine light flow through the arches of your feet and down toward the earth core.

The energy flowing out of your body touches the floor, penetrates the earth, layer by layer, and flows down further until it reaches the core of the earth.

• Channel your love and all positive things to the earth core.

 Let the earth return your love with a bright green light.

• While letting the divine light flow into the earth continuously, feel the bright green light from the earth start to flow up from the earth's surface.

The bright green light flows up like a cylinder that is the size of your body.

The energy reaches your lower body and climbs further. It reaches your buttocks, waist, solar plexus, chest, neck, cheeks, and the top of your head and climbs further.

After reaching a height of about 3 feet (1 meter) above your head, the bright green light starts to open like an umbrella to form the top portion of a giant egg that will give you protection.

• The bright green light flows continuously from the earth upwards through your body. The top portion of the giant egg flows down further and reaches the height of your head at a distance of about 3feet (1 meter) around your body.

 The top portion of the egg extends downwards further, reaching the height of your face, neck, chest, solar plexus, abdomen, waist, buttocks, and down further until it reaches the floor. Finally, the giant egg closes at about 3 feet (1meter) below your body. The giant egg is now completely formed and it will give you protection.

• As soon as the green egg is formed, the bright light that flows through your crown chakra only flows to your heart chakra.

The bright green light from the earth also flows up only to the heart chakra. At the heart chakra, the two lights mix and then flow in all directions through your whole body giving positive things to your life and your health.

• Now, have the intention that although you stop practicing this exercise, both energies will keep flowing continuously.

• Move your fingers and open your eyes with a smile.

Self Healing basic position

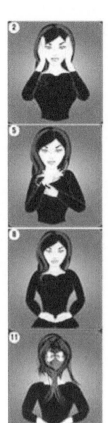
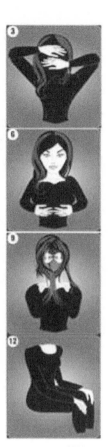

Other Healing

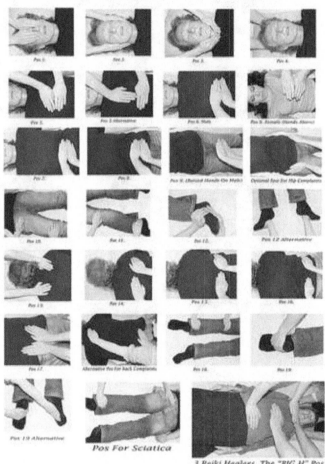

Reiki I Hand Positions

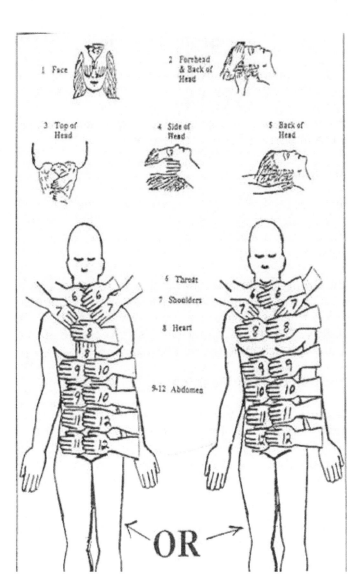

Group Healing

Group healing normally gives better results. Thus, if you are a beginner or if you have a client with a serious illness, or just for practice, you may find it beneficial to channel healing in a group. In group healing, there are three important factors to take note of :

Group Leader

One practitioner must be appointed as the leader. The group leader is responsible for the activation of the client's crown chakra and the opening of the client's aura before channeling energy.

The group leader gives the instructions to change hand positions in sequence and reminds all practitioners in the group to keep their energy synchronized with the leader's energy. The group leader will also sweep the aura after the energy channeling is finished.

Division of Body Positions

Because a group healing can be done by 2, 3, 4, 5 or more persons, you must assign a body position to each group member before energy channeling starts. This division of the client's body is done in order to not confuse the group members as to which body positions they should channel Reiki energy to next.

If there are more practitioners needed to cover each area of the client's body, each practitioner can just channel energy to the client without directing it to a certain position on the client's body.

In the following illustrations, you can see several examples of position divisions for 2, 3, 4, and 5 or more practitioners. Remember that the divisions in the illustration are only suggestions; you can divide the positions as you wish.

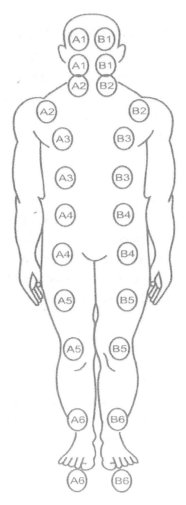

Two practitioners divide the hand positions on a client's left and right sides of the body. A1 represents the left and right palms of the first practitioner for the first position, A2 for the second position, and so forth. At the same time, the second practitioner channels energy at the positions indicated by B, that is, B1, B2, and so forth.

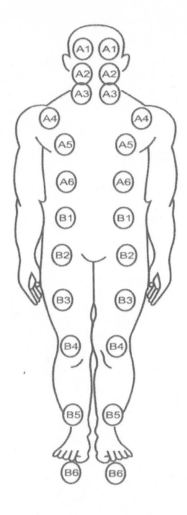

Two practitioners divide the hand positions on a client at the top and bottom parts of the body.

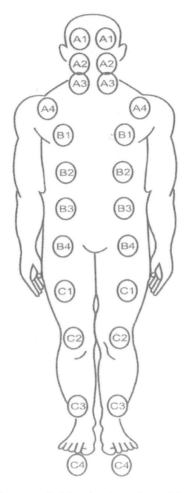

Three practitioners divide the hand positions along a client's body. Positions indicated by A are for the first practitioner, B for the second practitioner and C for the third. The number following the letter is the sequence of hand positions in channeling energy. So A1 (2 positions), B1(2 positions) and C1 (2 positions) are six hand positions for the first position and performed at the same time by the three practitioners.

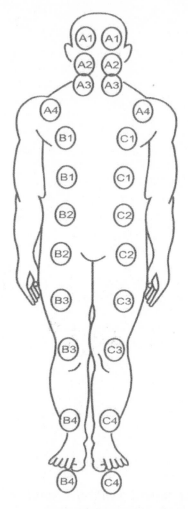

Three practitioners divide the hand positions on a client's body. The group leader handles the upper part of the client's body and the other members handle 2/3 of the lower part of the left and right sides of the client's body.

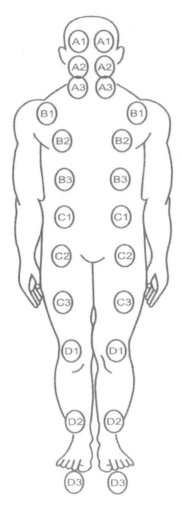

Four practitioners divide the hand positions along a
Client's body.

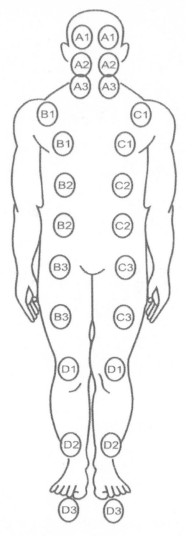

Alternative hand position division for a group healing composed of four practitioners.

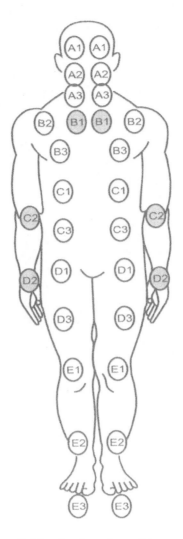

Five practitioners divide the hand positions along a client's body. The standard position division is not sufficient, so additional positions (with darker indicators) are added. Please note that these additional positions are only suggestions. If the client does not have any serious problem, the number of positions can be reduced. Additional positions which are different from these examples can be done at other body parts.

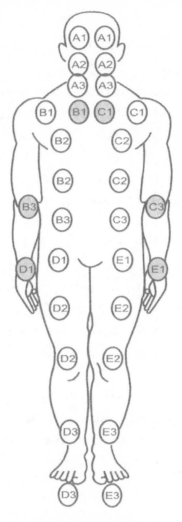

Alternative hand positions in a group of five practitioners. Even though there are many possibilities of hand position divisions with five practitioners in a group, the example shown in this illustration is the most common one used

Energy Synchronization

In a group healing, it is necessary for the group leader to always remind the other practitioners to synchronize their energy with the leader's energy. If the energy is not synchronized, not only will the energy cycles not happen, but also the result obtained will be very poor.

Energy from all the practitioners in the group will flow against one another causing the practitioners to become tired.

Also, the client will not receive the energy well. If good synchronization cannot be obtained in your group, it is better to change the group member who is tense or just channel energy individually not in a group.
Usually the energy in a group healing is not synchronized because of tension in one or more of the practitioners.

Fortunately, group energy can be synchronized quite easily. The group leader needs only to remind the group to synchronize their energy by simple intention. All practitioners must synchronize their energy with the group leader every time they move their hands to a new position.
Sometimes though, practitioners may be too tense to do that.

After you reach level 3, you will learn how to take control of the energy synchronization in a group healing.

So even though one or more in the group may be tense and unable to synchronize their energy to the group leader's, you can still synchronize the group's energy either when you are acting as a group leader or not.

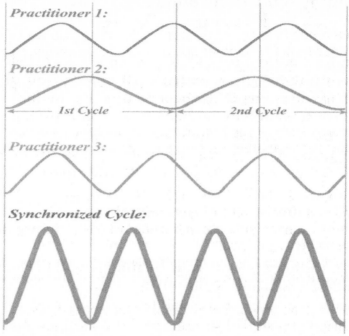

Individual energy cycle and synchronized energy cycle, In a synchronized group, every member has the same pattern of energy cycle which is shorter in duration, but higher in amplitude (stronger energy pressure) compared to an individual energy cycle.

Reiki for Animals and Plants

All living beings require energy and the energy has a major influence on their state of health.

Thus, REIKI energy is beneficial for animals and plants. You can channel energy to them by directing your palms to the animals or plants you want to channel the energy to.

Energy Cycle

Understanding more about the cycle of REIKI energy is important.

Knowing the cycle properly will enable you to sense when to stop the energy channeling to get the best results. In channeling energy, time may not be as accurate as the cycle because the energy being channeled is influenced by many variables, such as the condition of the client, the condition of your heart, your energy channeling condition, etc.

However when you observe the energy cycle you can know clearly what the energy is doing on the part of the body that is being treated. Understanding more about the cycle will enable you to know several significant matters, such as:

• Whether you are relaxed or not during channeling. If you are tense, the cycle will not happen.
• Whether the energy in a group healing is synchronized or not. If it is not synchronized, the cycle will not happen.
• Whether the energy channeled to one body position is sufficient or not. The shape and the period of the cycle will change with the increasing amount of energy channeled.

Frequently Asked Questions and Answers

• If I channel REIKI energy in bed, will the energy stop flowing as soon as I fall asleep?

The continuation of energy flow depends on two things: the stillness of your hands and how proper in the heart you are. If you move your hands either intentionally or not, before or after you fall asleep, the energy flow will stop. But if both hands stay still and in position, the energy will usually keep flowing for 10 to 15 minutes, depending on how proper in the heart you are and the energy requirement of the body part where your hands are positioned

• If both hands are positioned at only one location and the intention is to channel energy to the whole body, how will the energy flow to the whole body? Wasn't it mentioned that it is difficult for the energy to spread to the whole body due to blockages in our body?

Placing your hands at one position with intention to extend the energy to the whole body will cause the energy to spread around the body and then flow into the body from all directions (see Figure 1 below).

This is different from channeling energy to a position without intention to spread energy to the whole body. Although Reiki energy tries to extend all over the body, the energy enters the body from the point where the hands are positioned (see Figure 34b below). From that position, the energy is usually hindered by blockages so that the energy cannot reach the whole body.

Figure 1: Energy is channeled at the chest, but the intention is for the energy to spread to the whole body.

Figure 2: Energy is channeled at the chest without intention for the energy to spread to the whole body. The energy reaches a limited area.

• If it is possible to channel Reiki energy to the whole body by placing the hands at only one position, why is it still recommended to channel energy at many positions all over the body from head to feet?

When the hands are placed at only one position, but the intention is to spread energy to the whole body, the energy will cover the whole body surface and enter the body from almost all directions (see Figure 34aabove). Thus, the amount of energy that flows to each portion of the body is usually less and it is more difficult to reach deeper into the body.

• Does drinking water that has been treated with REIKI energy taste different?

Yes, usually the taste is slightly different. The most obvious is the different taste felt at the left and right sides of the tongue base.

• Are there any benefits in channeling Reiki energy to the medicines taken by a client?

Yes. it has been observed that medicines that have received Reiki energy give better results.

• How often should I practice the grounding technique?

Once a day is sufficient.

If you have spare time, it is better to channel energy to help others in healing

• I cannot see the energy as described in the grounding technique. What should I do?

After the REIKI attunement, you are connected with your higher consciousness. Your intention is sufficient so that channeling or directing energy will occur automatically and you do not have to visualize.

Thus, even though you cannot see the energy flowing, there is nothing to worry about. Just be relaxed.

• What will happen if I do chakra balancing but I channel energy to sets of chakras not as recommended?

Reiki energy will still cleanse the chakras, but balancing will not occur

• How often should the major chakra balancing technique be practiced?

It is recommended to practice chakra balancing at least once a week. If you have enough time, it is better if you can practice it daily.

Symbols

What Are Symbols?

In Reiki level 2 you learn about symbols, why they are used and how to use them.
A symbol is only a code used by a practitioner to give the specification of the energy type that you require. In this level, a practitioner will learn how to access and direct the energy with more precision.

As we know, there are different elements in the air such as nitrogen, oxygen, and other components. There are also different types of energy in the divine energy and each serves different purposes.

If you can access a specific type of energy in accordance to your need, you can expect better results in energy channeling/healing.
Since there are several types of energy, how do you access the specific type that you need?

Let's use an analogy.

If you are facing a group of students in a classroom and you want to communicate with a certain student, you can either call the name of the student or write down the name on a piece of paper and hold it up.

If the name is Mike, you either call "Mike" or write Mike"
What did you write when you wrote Mike? You wrote symbols. The word "Mike" consists of the symbols "M","I","K" and "E"

You will need to do the same when you want to access a specific type of energy in REIKI. You can either call or write the label (symbol).

Why do you want to use a certain type of energy? In level 2, you learn how to do cleansing, strengthening, and other specific healing functions.
For example, if you want to do a cleansing and use a "common" energy as in level 1, and the divine energy contains only N% cleansing energy, only N% of the divine energy is actually used for cleansing.

In order to cleanse or do other specific tasks more efficiently, you must access the specific type of energy that you require.

When doing a cleansing, use the cleansing energy type only. When you want to strengthen something, use the strengthening energy type.

There is nothing unusual about the symbols except that you are not accustomed to their usage yet. **The symbols themselves are not sacred. The symbols in Reiki do not have power.**

The source of the power is the divine blessing. Symbols are only used as codes or signs. In level 2, you learn to use the symbols solely as an aid. When you were a small child learning to stand up or walk, you needed something to hold onto to prevent you from falling.

After you could walk well and steadily, you did not need to hold onto anything. The same concept applies to the use of symbols.
After you have reached a certain level, you will no longer need to use the symbols.

The symbols might look odd to you. But imagine how strange the word "YOU" would be to a Chinese or ancient Indian person who does not know English, since they do not use a Latin alphabet. The combination of symbols "Y", "0", and "U" would look odd to them.

On the other hand, the symbols that mean "YOU" in Mandarin or Sanskrit will seem unusual to those of us who do not know these languages.

Some people are confused about the use of Reiki symbols. They mistakenly think that the symbols are sacred and that they can impart certain powers.
These people usually search for more symbols.

In their negative search, they sometimes obtain and use symbols that have negative characteristics and are not related to healing at all, Their desire to collect as many symbols as they can has diverted them toward other directions.

Meanwhile, the real goal of spiritual study, the real destiny of life is Simply to be closer to the Creator. Although you learn about and use symbols in level 2, do not consider the symbols sacred. You use the symbols to aid you in your learning process.

Remember that the core lesson in level 2 of Reiki is that you are well connected to the divine energy.
You can draw the symbols and retrieve the divine energy for the symbols you draw because you have this solid connection.

In the following sections of this book, please note that I use the phrase "retrieve the type of divine energy that is required with the symbol" or "symbol to retrieve energy" interchangeably.

The meaning is the same for both, Always remember that although the second sentence is used. i.e. "symbol to retrieve energy, it is not the symbol that has power, but it is you who has the capability to access the divine energy.

Function of the Symbols

As explained earlier, we use symbols in level 2 to specify the type of energy that we want to use to get a better result.
 By using symbols, we can:

•Get results more quickly
•Increase energy more easily
•Send energy beyond distance and time limitations
As a whole, we can say that the use of symbols increases the effectiveness of Reiki healing.

Three Primary Symbols in REIKI

Several symbols are used in REIKI. However, there are three symbols that are called primary symbols.
These are used in most energy channeling and they can be combined differently to obtain different results.

The three symbols are:
1. Cho-Ku-Rei
2. Sei-Hei-Ki
3. Hon-Sha-Se-Sho-Nen

Basic Components of Symbol

• Yantra

Yantra means drawing a symbol.
Reiki Practitioner II are only allowed to draw the symbols
by hand or using their five fingers.

The symbol must be memorized and drawn slowly and
correctly in accordance with symbol images in this book.

Practittioners can practice first by using pen and paper
before practicing it by hand

• Mantra

Mantra is the pronunciation of the symbol names that can
be carried out by intoning out loud or silenty.

In the procedure for using Reiki-Ho symbols, mantra
means the pronunciation of a symbol name 3 times in a
row

• Affirmation

Affirmation is a series of words/phrases that reflects the
purpose, intention, objective and expectation.

Affirmation plays an important role in the use of a Reiki-
Ho symbol.

1. Cho-Ku-Rei

Cho Ku Rei, is a symbol of Strength, reinforcement, protection, for sealing a process of treatment.
It Can strengthen other symbols. It is used for materialization

• To Strengthen the Energy Channeled
By drawing the Cho-Ku-Rei symbol before channeling energy at a designated position on the body, the energy flow becomes stronger.

• To Strengthen Another Symbol or a Program
The Cho-Ku-Rei symbol can also be used to strengthen the work of another symbol or a program (a combination of several symbols for a special purpose).

• To Cleanse, Activate, and Develop Chakras
By drawing the Cho-Ku-Rei symbol on a chakra, the chakra will become cleaner, more active, and more developed.
Thus, the Cho-Ku-Rei symbol is usually drawn on the palm chakras and the crown chakra before energy channeling to make the crown chakra, as the energy entrance, and the palm chakras, as the energy exit doors, cleaner, more active, and more developed.
 With this technique, you can channel energy better.

• To Cleanse Objects
Sometimes old objects have impure energy. To cleanse them, you can use the Cho-Ku-Rei symbol. You can also cleanse the energy in a room or a building with this symbol.

• For Physical Body Layers
In the spiritual context, we know that a human being has seven body layers. The Cho-Ku-Rei symbol is effective for common problems in the first body layer that consists of the physical body and its twin energy body

The standard Cho-Ku-Rei symbol is shown in Standard Cho-Ku-Rei symbol below, where the horizontal strip is on the left-hand side.
Because Reiki comes from a higher dimension where there is no space limitation, symbols can be reversed when drawing (see Reversed Cho-Ku-Rei symbol below).

In principle, there is no difference in function between the standard symbol and the reversed symbol, but it is recommended that you draw the symbol as used during your attunement ,that is, the standard symbol.

Standard Cho-Ku-Rei Symbol

Reversed Cho-Ku-Rei Symbol

It is easy to draw the Cho-Ku-Rei symbol. Before you begin, note the sequence numbers and arrows in Figure 36 below which indicate how to draw this symbol.

You only have to note that the spiral is quite symmetrical and the vertical line is in the middle of the spiral.

 Although it is recommended that this symbol have three and a half circles, you can draw slightly fewer or more without influencing the symbol's function.

It is more important to keep the symbol symmetrical.

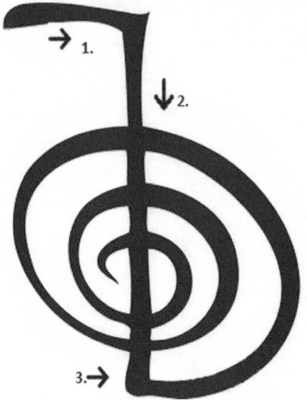

How to draw the Cho-Ku-Rei symbol

2. Sei-Hei-Ki

SHK is a symbol used for cleaning on of negative energy,
either in the body (in healing), or against objects, rooms,
etc.
It work the Mental-Emotional level, so as to use for the
treatment of the matters associated with the
Subconscious.

• Cleanses Negative Energy
With the Sei-Hei-Ki symbol, negative energy can be easily swept from the body.

For best results, this symbol is used at the position on the body with problems in order to sweep the negative energy out before channeling energy to that position.

• Cleanses and Balances the Petals of a Chakra
If the Cho-Ku-Rei symbol works on the chakra quantitatively, the Sei-Hei-Ki symbol works qualitatively.

After the chakra is cleansed, activated, and developed by the Cho-Ku-Rei symbol, then it is cleansed and balanced by the Sei-Hei-Ki symbol, and further improved by the Hon-Sha-Se-Sho-Nen symbol (see details under the section: Hon-Sha-Se-Sho-Nen Symbol" below).

• For Emotional Body Layers
This symbol is also very useful for common problems in the emotional body layer, which is the second body layer. Most negative emotions are accumulated here.

By cleansing this body layer, the accumulation of negative emotions is reduced.

For those who have emotional problems, it is recommended that the Sei-Hei-Ki symbol be used at the ajna chakra.

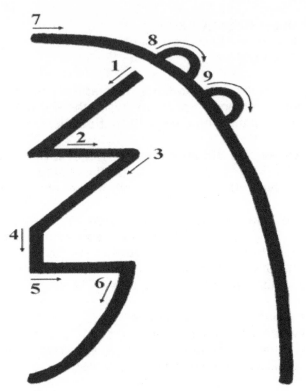

The Sei-Hei-Ki symbol and how to draw it

3. Hon-Sha-Se-Sho-Nen

HSZSN is a symbol used to send reiki across the dimensions of space and time, it is used for the delivery of energy at long distance, during the process of treatment and attunement.

The Hon-Sha-Se-Sho-Nen symbol eliminates limitations of distance, time, quantity, and so on.
 This symbol is very important in distant energy channeling and in the more complicated directing of energy you learn in level 3.

The functions of this symbol are :

• As a Channel for Sending Energy Distantly (Distance Relativity)

When sending energy distantly in level 1, Some of you may have experienced problems such as inaccuracy in reaching the target (for example you wanted to send energy to the abdomen, but the energy hit the chest) or energy that does not reach the receiver a full 100%.

By using the Hon-Sha-Se-Sho-Nen symbol as a channel, the two problems can be overcome easily.
However, do not expect to do distant energy channeling perfectly on the first try. You need to practice several times before you can do it well and achieve good results.

• Quantity Relativity

By using this symbol, a practitioner can channel energy to many targets at once. Thus, you can channel energy to 10, 100, 1000, or one million people at once without any limitation.

In level 2, the energy you send is divided. Thus, if you send energy to 10 people or objects, each receiver obtains 1/10 of the energy you channel.

But, after you complete level 3, when all your major chakras will be opened, you will be able to channel energy without limitation. You can channel energy to 10, 100, 1000 or one million people and each receiver will obtain fully 100% of the energy you channel.

• Time Relativity

It seems illogical to many people for someone to say that energy can be sent into the past or into the future. Fortunately, this possibility has been studied and confirmed by quantum physics.

Scientists now admit that in the higher dimensions time is in the shape of an ellipse, so it can turn forward or backward.

Since Reiki energy originates n a higher dimension it can easily transcend the limitations of time.

Using this symbol, energy can be sent to a specified moment after or before the time when the energy is actually being sent.

• Opening the Chakra Centers
Using the Hon-Sha-Se-Sho-Nen symbol can complete the cleansing of a chakra by Cho-Ku-Rei and Sei-Hei-Ki symbols.

 If the Cho-Ku-Rei and Sei-Hei-Ki work more on the petals of the chakra, the Hon-Sha-Se-Sho-Nen symbol works further to cleanse and open the center of the chakra.

• For the Mental Body Layer
This symbol is very useful for overcoming problems located in the third body layer or the mental body layer. Problems related with trauma are usually located in the mental body layer.

By using the Hon-Sha-Se-Sho-Nen symbol you can cleanse traumas in yourself or your clients.

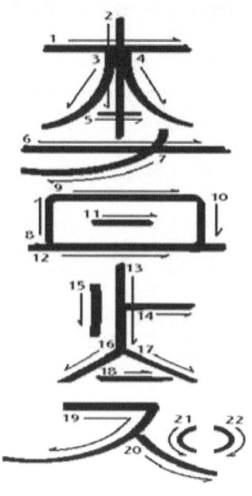

The Hon-Sha-Se-Sho-Nen symbol and how to draw it

Steps in Using the Symbols

You need to know the proper steps in using symbols so you can achieve maximum benefits from them.

Symbols are used to refer to specific types of divine energy. You have to allow sufficient time for the symbols to accumulate the type of energy you want before you can use the energy.

The following steps allow you to use the symbols properly:

1. Where
When drawing a symbol, you must draw the symbol near the body part that needs the treatment. As an example, when you want to cleanse negative energy from a client's elbow, you do not draw the symbol on your palms or on the client's crown chakra.

Instead, you should draw it near the client's elbow. Since the symbol you draw will retrieve the divine energy and form an energy ball, it is better if you draw the symbol at about 4 inches (10 cm)* above or in front of the body part that you are working on.
*)1 inch=2.5 cm

2. Choose a Proper Symbol
Choose the symbols according to your needs. Different symbols serve different purposes.

3. Drawing Method
Use five fingers pressed together or with all tips touching one another for the best result.

4. Connect
Let the divine energy (according to the symbol you have drawn) flow down until it forms an energy ball.
For best results, intend to retrieve energy for the symbol simply by calling the symbol's name several times(usually three times is sufficient, but there is no limitation).

Also, have the intention that the energy for your symbol flows down.
Do it in a relaxed way without forcing. For example, "Divine energy suitable for Cho-Ku-Rei please descend into this Cho-Ku-Rei."

5. Wait
Divine energy will start flowing down. Wait until a dense energy ball is formed.
It is better for you to place one or both palms facing the symbol at about 4 inches (10 cm) away from the symbol.

That way you can feel, by the pressure on your palms, if the divine energy has formed an energy ball.

6.Push the Collected Energy Ball into the Body
Push the energy ball into the body area that requires the energy.
Have the intention that the whole energy ball enters the body, even if the body portion is smaller in size than the energy ball.

7. Give Directions

Due to the fact that certain types of energy can be used for several purposes, it is important to give exact directions.
The important thing when you give directions is the connection between your heart and the energy.

Since you have just started to use your heart, your connection to your heart may not be there all the time. For this reason, it is recommended to give directions two to three times.

The figures below illustrate the specific steps to follow in using symbols:

Draw the symbol around 4 inches (10 cm) above the body part that needs energy channeling. In this example, it is above a client's stomach.

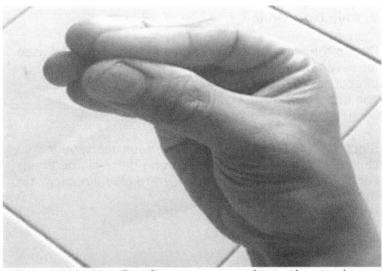

Figure 39b: Use five fingers squeezed together to draw the symbol

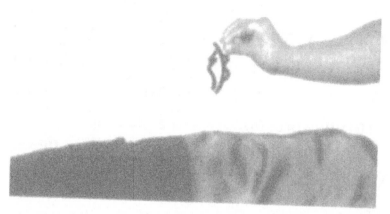

Draw the symbol above the stomach with the center of the drawing around 4 inches (10 cm) above the stomach

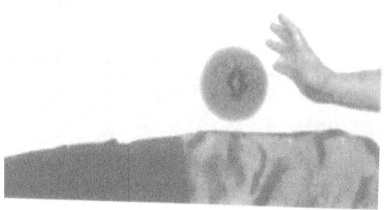

Connect and Wait: Let the kind of divine energy that is needed flow down until it forms a dense energy ball

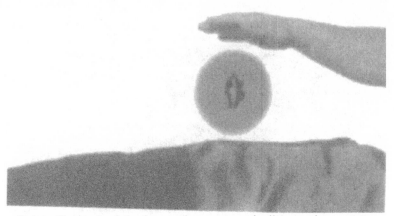

Bring the palm(s) above the energy ball in order not to break it

Push the energy ball into the targeted area, in this case into the stomach.

Give direction or affirmation to the energy ball with the palm(s) still facing the energy ball that has been pushed into the target area.

Drawing Symbols with Five Fingers

Symbols can be drawn using several methods. They are:
• Using only one finger (on every fingertip there is a small chakra)
• Using two fingers or more
• Using the palm chakras
• Using major chakras
• Using intention only

At this stage you are a beginner in using symbols. Therefore, to achieve the best result, it is recommended that you use five fingers squeezed together neatly.

If you use only one finger, the energy that flows out through the mini chakra on the fingertip is very little. It is like drawing with a slender pencil on a very large piece of paper. The drawing will be too thin.

You must use something thicker. It is best to squeeze your five fingertips together neatly so that the symbol drawing will be thick and dense.

If your fingertips are not squeezed together neatly, the drawing formed will not be neat. It is like drawing using a brush with split bristles.

If you use the palm chakras, the energy flowing through will be too flat and too wide. Drawing the symbol with major chakras is not safe because the major chakras are too close to important internal organs.

If you use the last option, that is using intention only, you may be using your mind too much while one of the main goals of Reiki is to prepare you for advanced spiritual study by being in your heart more.

After looking at the available choices and the advantages and disadvantages of each option, it is recommended that you use your five fingers to draw symbols in order to get the optimum results at this stage.

Things to Note in Drawing Symbols

Many people will still make mistakes in drawing symbols even though they have been given the seven steps explained above.

For this reason, the methods for drawing symbols will be discussed further. The additional discussion will give you a better understanding of symbol drawing. with this understanding you will recognize what is important and what is not important.

For example, the term "connect" in point 4 above is only an example of a word that can be used. You can use other terms like "link" or any other term that you prefer. What is important in that step is that you direct the symbol to retrieve the divine energy.

On the other hand, the distance in drawing a symbol from the body is very important. If you draw a Cho-Ku-Rei symbol about ½ inch (1 cm) above the body surface, the energy ball formed will not be as good as when the symbol is drawn 4 inches (10 cm) above or in front of the body surface

1. Draw the Symbol Exactly Above or in Front of the Target

Although symbols are drawn about 4 inches (10 cm) from the target, the symbols must be drawn exactly above or in front of the target, not too much to the side.
By drawing the symbols at the center above the target, the whole energy ball can be pushed into the target easily. On the other hand, if the symbols are drawn too far from the center of the target, the energy ball might not be entirely pushed into the body.

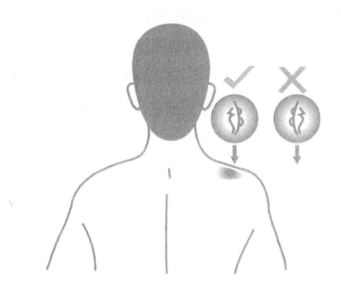

One symbol is drawn exactly above the target area and the other one is drawn too far to the side. In this case the target area is the shoulder

2. Choose a Suitable Symbol

You must use symbols that are suitable for your purpose. For example, you do not want to use a strengthening symbol when you want to cleanse impurities.
To cleanse impurities, you must use a symbol that is useful for cleansing.

3.Draw the Symbol Correctly

As discussed earlier, the best method to draw symbols is by using five fingers squeezed together neatly. Remember that you are drawing with energy that is invisible to most people.
If you draw the symbol with a pencil or pen on paper and the symbol drawing is not good, it can only be worse if you were to draw it and not be able to visually see it.

That is why we want to do our best by using the fingers to form one focus. This will give us better control and a stronger energy channel.

The symbol still works, whether you draw it perfectly or not. However, if the symbol drawing is good, the energy ball that forms will be better than if the drawing is poor. In drawing symbols, you do not have to worry about whether the symbol should be drawn straight or not.

Reiki energy comes from a higher dimension where there is no space limitation. This means that you can draw a Reiki symbol straight, slanted, upside down, and so on. As long as the symbol drawing is symmetrical, the symbol will work well.

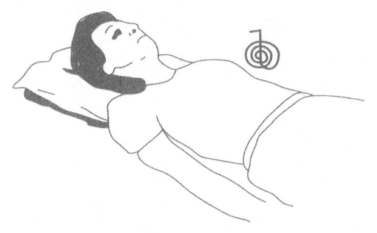

The symbol is drawn vertically

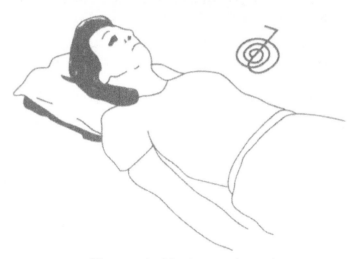

The symbol is drawn slanted

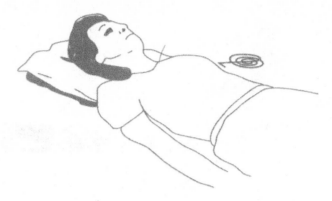

The symbol is drawn horizontally

4. Size of Energy Ball

The size of the energy ball depends on two important factors: the size of the symbol drawn and the distance between the symbol and the body.

The size of the symbol influences the size of the energy ball because the symbol becomes the core of the energy ball.
Imagine that you draw a symbol about one foot long.

The energy ball formed will be slightly larger than one foot in length and it will not be round, but oval. If you are not aware of this, you might push only part of the energy ball formed.

The symbol is drawn too close to the target area. The energy ball that forms is small and flattened.

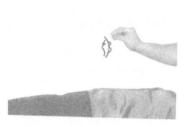

The symbol is drawn too far from the target area. The energy ball that forms is big and not dense enough.

If a symbol is too big, the energy ball formed will not be dense enough.

So it is best not to draw a symbol that is too large, because the size of the symbol influences the size of the subsequently formed energy ball (except in symbols that are required to be large or for a specific requirement)

According to our observations, we have found that it is best to form the energy ball with a diameter of about 8 inches (20 cm) so that the energy ball will be dense enough.

If the energy ball formed is too large, for instance, 30 inches (75 cm) in diameter, it will not be dense enough. Also, if the energy ball is too large, only part of the ball can usually be pushed into the section of the body in need and the other part will be wasted.

5. Do Not Block Energy from Above

After you have the intention to retrieve a specific type of energy, do not block the energy flowing down from above. If one or both of your hands block the energy, a longer time will be needed to form a dense energy ball.

It is recommended that you not block the energy flowing down from above. Not because the energy cannot change direction, but to get more effective results.

6.Wait until the Energy Ball is Quite Dense

Make sure that you have allowed for enough time to pass for the divine energy to flow down creating a dense energy ball.

You can feel this with your palms if you direct your palms toward the symbol at a distance of about 4 inches (10 cm). When the energy ball is quite dense, you can feel strong pressure from the energy ball.

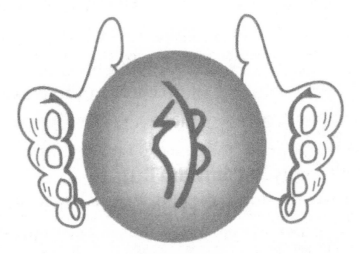

Waiting for the energy ball to form and sensing the energy ball correctly.

In sensing the energy pressure, you can move your palms slightly so that you can feel it better.

 But do not move your hands too close to the symbol drawn because you can ruin the energy ball.

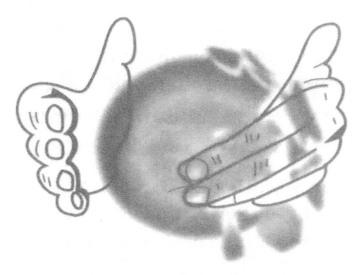

Incorrect way to sense the energy ball

Remember that with Reiki it is best to surrender.
Informing the energy ball for a symbol, you only need to
give direction to the symbol to retrieve divine energy.

After that, you just surrender.

Do not make any effort to retrieve more energy or to
make the energy balldenser because this will give you the
reverse effect.

7.Push the Whole Energy Ball into the Target

Although the energy ball formed is the proper size, about
8 inches (20cm) in diameter, when you push the energy
ball into the body part in need, have the intention for the
whole energy ball to go into the target.

For best results, please bear in mind the following:
• Sometimes the energy ball is big, such as the energy
ball for the whole body. Make sure that the whole energy
ball is absorbed by the entire body.

• Sometimes a standard energy ball is still bigger than the target, if used for a small body part such as the wrist.
• If you only push, the energy ball might penetrate through the target.

8. Directions

To achieve the desired result, you must give correct directions. You do not need to remember the exact wording of the instructions, as long as the instructions you give are correct.

9.Give Sufficient Time for the Symbol to Work
After the directions are given, the energy will start working.
The energy needs some time to do its task.
Allow the energy sufficient time to execute the directions you have given. Although, the energy works the strongest in the first 3-10 minutes, the energy will work for several hours afterwards.

Basic Procedure of Symbols

(1) Draw the symbol (yantra) slowly, correctly and proportionally in front of or on top of certain object. General size of these symbols drawings us around 10-20cm (height).

After drawing the symbol, place both palms on both sides of the symbol.

Note : keep your hands movements from damaging or removing the drawn symbol!

(2) Say the symbol name 3 times (mantra), and intend for the symbol to be connected with the original symbol,

Connected with divine energy, and then drawn the divine energy.

For example: "*Chokurei, Chokurei, Chokurei .... connects with the original symbol, connects with the divine energy, and drawns the divine energy* ".

(3) Wait for about 10 seconds.

Those who are sensitive will be able to feel that the symbol will change into a dense ball of energy.

While those who have ability of clairvoyance will see that the symbol "lights up" like a neon light.

For those who are not sensitive, they can imagine that the symbol is surrounded by a spherical energy.

(4) Direct the energy ball slowly to the object

(5) Give affirmation.

(6) Finish

Application of Symbols

• Charging Energy (CKR)
Enter energy ball CKR to part of the body (usually the navel) or to specific objects (eg objects, food, etc..)

Give affirmation: *"Give energy evenly throughout the body / this object"*.

• Doubling Energy (CKR)
Enter CKR energy ball to part of the body (usually the navel) or to specific objects (eg objects, food, etc..)

Give affirmation: *"Double the energy in the body / object evenly"*

•Chakra activation (CKR)
This application should be carried out regularly everyday, and it is recommended to activate chakra before giving Reiki Treatment or when receiving Attunement.

It should be applied across the main Chakra and Palm chakra or at least in : Crown Chakra, Hearts Chakra, and Palm Chakra.
The patient in Reiki-Treatment should apply this chakra activation.

Enter CKR energy ball into chakra in question. Give Affirmation: *"Open, Clean, and activate chakras (.........)*

•Clearing Negative Energy (SHK)

Create large energy ball Seiheiki (throughout the patient's body), enter the energy ball into the patient's body.

Give Affirmation: *"Clear all the negative energy, and all the negative elements in the patient's body"*

Note: Seiheiki symbol, can be reinforced with Chokurei symbol.

Seiheiki symbol, can also be used to clear the negative elements in a room / place.

Seiheiki symbol can be used for local cleansing (certain body parts).

•Distance Energy Transfer (HSSZN).

Honshazeshonen symbol acts as an energy mediator between giver and receiver.

By using Honshazeshonen symbol at the beginning of giving energy, it will form "a path" of communication between the giver and receiver. Where as if the energy receiver "is physically pulled" before the energy giver

procedure:
create Honshazeshonen energy ball in front of the body (chest).

Hold the Honshazeshonen energy ball , while saying affirmation of distance energy transfer, for example:

"All the symbols and energy are intended to Mr. X in city B, and will work now"

Next, transfer the energy and symbols like direct healing. Use visualization or tools (puppet, your own body, etc..)./

Note: Affirmation: *".... Will work now .. "can be changed in accordance with the purposes, for example:" ... will work at 22.00 ... "or" ... will work if he or she is ready to receive energy ... "*

- Balancing Emotion

Humans in everyday life can not be separated from emotional events, such as : sadness, joy, anger, fear, etc.

Emotion release can be hampered due to several things, resulting in emotional accumulation in the subconscious.

Furthermore, there are many cases indicating that physical illness is often caused by these emotional accumulations.

Emotional balancing can be carried out through Reiki because it can release emotional accumulations in the subconscious.

The process of balancing emotion through Reiki requires a relatively long time, that is between half an hour to two hours, so that good preparations are needed, such as relatively quiet place, relaxed channeling position, and so on.

The process of balancing these emotions will result in the release of a variety of emotions from the subconscious coming out with various reactions, such as laughing, crying, angry, and so on

All of these reactions to emotion must be completely released, in accordance with the objective of balancing this emotion.

Therefore, it is strongly recommended that the healer can provide a deep understanding to the patient of the reactions that may arise and what should be done by the patient

- Procedure for Balancing Emotions

First, direct Seiheiki energy ball into Ajna Chakra (without affirmation).
Then, direct Chokurei energy ball into Ajna Chakra (Without affirmation).
Next, direct Seiheiki energy ball to the back of the head (without affirmation).
 After that, direct Chokurei energy ball to the back of the head (without affirmation)

Channel the energy with both palms, where one palm on Ajna Chakra and another palm on the back of the head. Intend that you will channel the energy for balancing emotions.

Note: all patient emotions that may arise must be completely removed. The new process is stopped if the patient is feeling fresh and free from any emotional turmoil.

- Psychic Protection

In addition to healing, the Reiki can be used to build a psychic protection on an object.

Procedure:
Create Chokurei energy ball in front of the chest. Then hold the energy ball, and visualize that the object to be protected is in the energy ball.

Give affirmation: "*This powerful energy ball will protect [object, person] from all things and negative forces. No negative energy can penetrate this ball, but all positive energy can easily penetrate the ball. The energy ball will last for [...] day*".

Remove the energy ball, and don't ever think about it again.

Note: The resistance of this energy ball depends on the level of practitioner's soul awareness.

In general, novice practitioners can commonly form energy ball that can last between 1 hour - 3 days.

Therefore, it is recommended that the practitioners periodically replaces the energy ball.

•Materialization

In the spiritual, it is known that a continuously visualized desire (non-physical effort) will affect the macrocosmic system, and it is not impossible to make that desire come true (materialized) with a logical cause and effect when the materialization occurs.

The intended desire can be anything, including material, condition, etc

In western theory, another form of this method is known in various terminologies and variations,

Including: positive mental attitude, utilization of the subconscious ability, harnessing the right brain, etc

In Reiki, a practitioner can harness the power of Reiki symbol to help continuous visualization of a desire, so that it can be materialized. The intended symbol is Chokurei symbol.

Procedure:
First, create Chokurei energy ball in front of the chest.
then, say Positive Affirmation: *"I am happy because (...)"*

Repeat the affirmation at least 4 times with sincerity and depth of heart.

Remove the energy ball into the universe (cosmos), and do not think about the energy ball.

The ball travels to Macrocosmos system in its own way.

Repeat the procedure everyday

Daikomio
Reiki Master Symbol for Attunement

Attunement

Preparation ;

• Connect to Spiritual Being:

Pray to God Almighty. Ask for help from Spiritual Counsellor I: High Spirit, Reiki Guide, Ascended Master, Etc..

•Open Reiki Channel:

Enter Chokurei energy ball to Palms Chakra, Chakra Crown, and Heart Chakra.

•Cleansing:

Clean the Attunement room by sending Chokurei energy ball to six sides of the room, and the center of the room.

• Make an intention about the Attunement level to be provided.

REIKI LEVEL 1 - STEP-BY-STEP Of ATTUNEMENT PROCEDURE

Purpose of Attunement The main purpose of an attunement or reiju (pronounced Ray-joo) is to raise the student's energy level to re-connect to the true inner self (soul), plus strengthen the connection to universal spiritual energy.

In Reiki Level 1, the student is attuned through four initiations, to three symbols ; the power symbol

Cho-Ku-Rei, the mental/emotional symbol Sei-He-Ki

and the
distant/absentee symbol Hon-Sha-Ze-Sho-Nen.

1st initiation
2nd initiation
3rd initiation
4th initiation

Energy is utilized through student's physical body to raise energy vibrational level and to increase healing capacity.

Attunement opens crown chakra to access and channel more universal energy light, plus initiate universal wisdom and purpose to flow Energy, operating through student's etheric body (spiritual double located slightly above the physical body).

Attunement opens cervical and spinal column to improve the functioning of entire nervous system, plus open throat chakra to enhance communication.

Balances studen't right and left brain for clearer thinking and action .

Influences student's pineal and pituitary glands, which increase higher consciousness and intuition.

The pineal gland located at the 7th chakra (crown) increases perception of light, plus connects student to the universal source of energy.

The pituitary gland located at the 6th chakra (third eye) is also influenced to balance the endocrine system (see diagram page 19), as well as the brain.

The symbols are permanently sealed into the student's hands and aura, before the energies between student and Master, are disconnected.

This initiation completes the process allowing the energy channels to remain open.

Preparing Students for Attunement Process (to relax student)

• Play soft Reiki music

• Sit with feet flat on the floor, place hands on laps (avoid crossing limbs – this indicates non acceptance for receiving)

• Close your eyes, take 3-deep breaths and relax

• Take a moment to scan yourself

• Starting at your feet and working upward toward your crown, observe any tenseness and relax each muscle

• Say to students, "You are safe and secure at all times"

• Begin guided meditation to relax them
Procedure during Attunement

• Ring bell/gong 3times for student to enter attunement room
When student enters the attunement room they will bow to Reiki Master (to show respect)

• Bow to picture of Usui sensei (to show respect)

• Sit on stool with back straight, but comfortable

• Feet flat on floor (avoid crossing legs this indicates non-acceptance for receiving)

•Hands held loosely on lap (avoid crossing hands this indicates non-acceptance for receiving)

• Close eyes and relax

Guided Meditation Script BEFORE Attunement to Relax Student

• In front of you is a wide, staircase made of clear quartz crystal

• Walk over to the staircase until you are standing in front of it

• As I count from 1 to 10, I want you to climb the stairs until you reach the landing at the top

• 1 and 2 and 3 and 4 and 5 and 6 and 7 and 8 and 9 and 10

• You are now standing on the landing and in front of you is a white door

• Slowly walk over to the door and open it, then step over the threshold

• Remember, you are safe and secure at all times

• Before you is a beautiful, serene park, full of lush green trees and fragrant, colourful blooming flowers in all shape and sizes

• Their heady aroma permeates the air around you
• In front of you is a slide situated in front of a large pool filled with rainbow coloured water

• Walk over to the slide and as I count from 1 to 7, climb the stairs – 1 and 2 and 3 and 4 and 5 and 6 and 7

• Now sit down on the slide, don't worry about being fully dressed, just slide down into the water below

• Relax in the water, feel its invigorating, refreshing, crisp, coolness as it laps against your skin

• As you float and relax, be aware of what healing colour your body naturally absorbs

• Above you is the yellow glow of the afternoon sun, beating its warmth over you

• You feel so relaxed, so peaceful and very happy

• Stay in the water and enjoy yourself

• When you hear the bell ring three times, you will be ready to receive your attunement

• If it's your turn, slowly open your eyes, get up out of your chair and meet me at the door of the healing room

Guided Meditation AFTER Attunement

• You have now received attunement to Reiki level 1 and you will experience this in your own unique way

• You are feeling very relaxed and very peaceful

• Feel and know that the energy and power from the Reiki symbols are penetrating the very essence of your soul

• Feel and know that you are a very loving and powerful channel for the Reiki healing energy

• Feel and know that you are a powerful healing facilitator who will only perform Reiki for the highest good for self and others

• Know that your spirit healing team will assist you whenever you call upon their help and guidance

• Now I am going to count from 1 to 5 and when I reach number 5, you will return to the present time, take 3-deep breaths, open your eyes and you will feel very refreshed, plus invigorated

• 1...start to come back.....2.....you are slowly returning to conscious awareness.....3....4..... you are almost back......5....you are fully back in the present time.......take 3-deep breaths.....open your eyes......rub your fingers together......you are fully conscious and aware of the present

• If you feel unsteady or dizzy, take 3-deep breaths, drink some water or touch an inanimate object to help ground yourself.

Attunement to Reiki Level 1 is processed through four initiations.

First Initiation (Energy operates through student's physical body to raise energy vibrational level and to increase healing capacity.

Attunement opens crown chakra to access and channel more universal energy light, plus initiate universal wisdom and purpose to flow)

Position: Back of Student; Area – Shoulders and Crown
Stand behind student and place your right hand on student's shoulder.

Connect your energy to the universal energy source by raising your left arm with hand facing upward (to receive universal energy) and visualize or draw the Master

Symbol Dai-Ko-Myo (pronounced Die-Coe-Me-Oh) above the student's crown.

With your left arm still raised, place your right hand on top of student's crown and silently say a prayer or invocation

(E.g. "I ask for universal blessings from spirit and the Reiki healing team to assist this student to become a compassionate, loving Reiki healer who will be filled with humility in order to serve humanity for the highest good")

Cup your hands, like a funnel, over student's crown, but leave a small opening for a blowing hole

Position your tongue, take 3-deep belly/kidney breaths and contract your Hui-Yin.

Visualize white light entering your crown, going through your tongue, down the front of your body to the Hui Yin point, then back up your spine to the centre of your head (**Fire Dragon energy**)

Blow "*Fire Dragon*" energy into student's crown

As you are blowing, visualize and silently intone each symbol 3times

Cho-Ku-Rei 3times (ChohKoo-Ray)

Hon-Sha-Ze-Sho-Nen 3times (Hon-ShawZay-Show-Nen)

Sei-He-Ki 3times (SayHay-Key)

See the symbol penetrate into student's heart, then along their arms to their hands; wait until you feel the process is completed before continuing – use your intuition.

Note: Release your Hui Yin after the blowing is completed

Second Initiation (Energy operates through student's etheric body (which is spiritual double located slightly above the physical body).

Attunement opens cervical and spinal column to improve the functioning of entire nervous system, plus open the throat chakra to enhance communication)

Position:
Back of Student; Area – Both Shoulders
Continue standing behind student and place one hand on each shoulder, position your tongue, take 3-deep belly/kidney breaths and contract your Hui-Yin Visualize

and silently intone Cho-Ku-Rei (Choh-Koo-Ray) 3times, as you blow "Fire Dragon" energy into each shoulder.

See the symbol move along student's cervical and spinal column; wait until you feel the process is completed before continuing – use your intuition.

Note: Release your Hui Yin after the blowing is completed

Third Initiation (Balances student's right and left brain for clearer thinking and action)

Position: Back of Student; Area – Occipital Ridge at Back of Head Continue standing behind student and place your thumbs on and parallel to their occipital ridge (where the back of the head meets the neck), then position your tongue, take 3-deep belly/kidney breaths and contract your Hui-Yin while blowing.

As you blow, visualize

and silently intone Cho-Ku-Rei (Choh-Koo-Ray) 3times. See the symbol penetrate the back of the head; wait until you feel the process is completed before continuing use your intuition.

Note: Release your Hui Yin after the blowing is completed

Fourth Initiation (Influences student's pineal and pituitary glands, increasing higher consciousness and intuition.

This initiation completes the process allowing the energy channels to remain open)

Position: Right Side of Student; Area – Forehead and Back of Head

Move to student's right side and place your left hand on the lowest part of the back of their head as you place your right hand across their forehead, position your tongue, then take 3-deep belly/kidney breaths and contract your Hui-Yin while blowing.

Visualize

and silently Intone Cho-Ku-Rei (Choh-Koo-Ray) 3times, as you blow the "Fire Dragon" energy into both areas (back of head and then forehead). See the symbol penetrate these areas; wait until you feel the process is completed before continuing – use your intuition.

Note: Release your Hui Yin after the blowing is completed

Final Step of 4th Initiation (Three major symbols are permanently sealed into student's hands where the energy is accessed automatically from the student's subconscious level)

Position: Kneel in Front of Student; Area – Both Hands Palms Up

Walk counter-clockwise to student's front. Kneel in front of student and place both their hands in open hand position (palms open and facing upward) on their lap.

Apply symbols to each hand separately. Starting with the left hand, cup your hands (like a funnel) over the palm, but leave a small opening in the centre to blow the symbols into

Position your tongue, take 3-deep belly/kidney breaths and contract your Hui-Yin while blowing the "Fire Dragon" energy into the 1st hand
As you blow, visualize

and silently intone Cho-Ku-Rei (Choh-Koo-Ray) 3times.
Then visualize

and silently intone Hon-Sha-Ze-Sho-Nen (Hon-Shaw-Zay-Show-Nen) 3times.
Lastly, visualize

and silently intone Sei-He-Ki (Say-Hay-Key) 3times

See the three symbols penetrate into the hand.

Note: Release your Hui Yin after the blowing is completed.

Keep the left palm open and facing upward as you repeat the same procedure to the right hand

Once the procedure is completed on both hands, with the palms still open, simultaneously with both your hands, gently tap both palms 3-times to seal the symbols in

Gently close their hands into loosely closed fists Criss-cross their hands across their heart and then criss-cross your hands over theirs Hold this position until you feel that the initiation is completed -use your intuition

When finished, walk counter-clockwise to back of student, bow to Usui sensei and give a silent prayer of gratitude,

(E.g. "I give thanks of gratitude to the Reiki healing team for all assistance received during this attunement – thank-you, thank-you, thank-you")

While at the back of the student, draw the Raku

symbol to ground and seal the symbols into the student's aura plus disconnect your energy from that of the student's

Ring bell 1-time (or advise student that attunement is completed)

Student bows first to Usui sensei, then to Reiki Master Teacher (to show respect), before leaving the room to return to their chair to continue meditating

When all attunements are completed, change from your attunement garment, do your cleansing exercise (E.g. dry brush or shower method) and wash hands (for sanitary purposes, plus to cleanse external energies)

Return to teaching room and use a guided meditation to bring students back to the present time

REIKI LEVEL 2 – STEP-BY-STEP ATTUNEMENT PROCEDURE

Purpose of Attunement The main purpose of an attunement or reiju (pronounced Ray-joo) is to raise your energy level to re-connect you to your inner true self (soul), plus strengthen your connection to universal spiritual energy.

In Reiki Level 2, you are attuned through one initiation process.

This opens your heart chakra, which allows you to share and experience un-conditional universal love and compassion.

Preparing Students for Attunement Process (to relax student)

• Play soft Reiki music

• Sit with feet flat on the floor, place hands on laps (avoid crossing limbs)

• Close your eyes, take 3-deep breaths and relax

• Take a moment to scan yourself

• Starting at your feet and working upward toward your crown, observe any tenseness and relax each muscle

• Say to students, "You are safe and secure at all times"

Procedure during Attunement

* Ring bell/gong 3times for student to enter attunement room

* When student enters the attunement room they will Bow to Reiki Master

Bow to Usui sensei (to show respect)

Sit on stool with back straight

Feet flat on floor (legs are not crossed)

Hands held loosely on lap (hands are not crossed)

Close eyes and relax

Guided Meditation Script to Relax Students

In front of you is a wide, staircase made of clear quartz crystal

• Walk over to the staircase until you are standing in front of it

• As I count from 1 to 10, I want you to climb the stairs until you reach the landing at the top

• 1 and 2 and 3 and 4 and 5 and 6 and 7 and 8 and 9 and 10

• You are now standing on the landing and in front of you is a white door

• Slowly walk over to the door and open it, then step over the threshold

• Remember, you are safe and secure at all times

- Before you is a beautiful, serene park, full of lush green trees and fragrant, colourful blooming flowers in all shape and sizes

- Their heady aroma permeates the air around you
- In front of you is a slide situated in front of a large pool filled with rainbow coloured water

- Walk over to the slide and as I count from 1 to 7, climb the stairs – 1 and 2 and 3 and 4 and 5 and 6 and 7

- Now sit down on the slide, don't worry about being fully dressed, just slide down into the water below

- Relax in the water, feel its invigorating, refreshing, crisp, coolness as it laps against your skin

- As you float and relax, be aware of what healing colour your body naturally absorbs

- Above you is the yellow glow of the afternoon sun, beating its warmth over you

- You feel so relaxed, so peaceful and very happy

- Stay in the water and enjoy yourself

- When you hear the bell ring three times, you will be ready to receive your attunement

- If it is your turn, slowly open your eyes, get up out of your chair and meet me at the door of the healing room

Student is attuned through one initiation to open their heart chakra, which allows them to share and experience unconditional universal love and compassion.

1

2

3

4

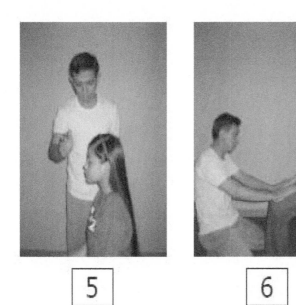

5

6

7

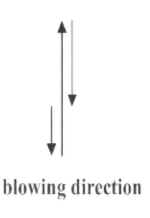

blowing direction

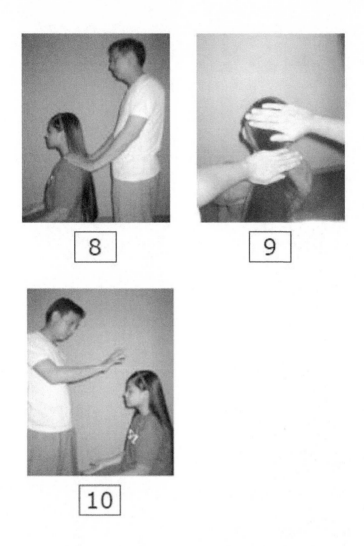

Step 1 - Position: Back of Student; Area Shoulders and Crown

Stand behind student and place your right hand on student's shoulder.

Connect your energy to the universal energy source by raising your left arm with hand facing upward (to receive universal energy) and visualize or draw the Master Symbol Dai-Ko-Myo

(pronounced Die-Coe-Me-Oh) above the student's crown.

With your left arm still raised, place your right hand on top of student's crown and silently say a prayer or invocation.

(E.g. *"I ask for universal blessings from spirit and the Reiki healing team to assist this student to become a compassionate, loving Reiki healer who will be filled with humility in order to serve humanity for the highest good"*)

Cup your hands, like a funnel, over student's crown, but leave a small opening for a blowing hole

Position your tongue, take 3-deep belly/kidney breaths and contract your Hui-Yin. Visualize white light entering your crown, going through your tongue, down the front of your body to the Hui Yin point, then back up your spine to the centre of your head (Fire Dragon energy)

Blow the "Fire Dragon" energy into the student's crown
As you are blowing, visualize and silently intone each symbol 3times

Cho-Ku Rei 3times (ChohKoo-Ray)

Hon-Sha-Ze Sho-Nen 3times (Hon-ShawZay-Show-Nen)

Sei-He-Ki 3times (SayHay-Key)

See the symbols penetrate into student's heart and then along their arms to their hands; wait until you feel the process is completed before continuing.

Note: Release your Hui Yin after the blowing is completed

Step 2 - Position: Kneel in Front of Student; Area Hands in Prayer Position

Walk counter-clockwise to student's front, place student's hands in prayer (Japanese call this gassho, pronounced gas-hoe) position and then cup your hands, in prayer position, around student's hands with your own finger tips touching each other like a pyramid (called little cup)

Visualize

and intone silently 3times Cho-Ku-Rei (Choh-Koo-Ray).

Then visualize

and intone silently 3times Hon-Sha-Ze-Sho-Nen (Hon-Shaw-Zay Show-Nen).

Lastly, visualize and intone silently 3times Sei-He-Ki (Say Hay-Key)

Step 3 - Position: Kneel in Front of Student;

Area – Left Hand on Heart While still at student's front, place student's left hand over their heart and have them keep it there while you sandwich their right hand between yours (one above and one below)
First, visualize

and intone out loud 3times Cho-Ku-Rei (Choh-Koo-Ray)
 Next, visualize

and intone out loud 3times HonSha-Ze-Sho-Nen (HonShaw-Zay-Show-Nen)

Lastly, visualize

and intone out loud 3times Sei-HeKi (Say-Hay-Key)

Step 4 - Position: Kneel in Front of Student;

Area – Hands in Prayer, Hold with Left Hand over HeartWhile still at student's front, place student's hands again in prayer (Japanese call this gassho, pronounced gas-hoe) position and hold with your left hand; place your right hand over
student's heart.

Then with your left hand press student's hands (still in prayer position) against your right hand.

First, visualize

and intone out loud 3times Cho-Ku-Rei (Choh-Koo-Ray)
Next, visualize

and intone out loud 3times HonSha-Ze-Sho-Nen
(HonShaw-Zay-Show-Nen)
Lastly, visualize

and intone out loud 3times Sei-HeKi (Say-Hay-Key)
Step 5 - Position: Kneel in Front of Student; Area – Right Hand on Heart

While still at student's front, place student's right hand over their heart and have them hold it there.

Then sandwich student's left hand between yours (one above and one below)

First, visualize

and intone out loud 3times Cho-Ku-Rei (Choh-Koo-Ray)
Next, visualize

and intone out loud 3times HonSha-Ze-Sho-Nen (HonShaw-Zay-Show-Nen)

Lastly, visualize

and intone out loud 3times Sei-HeKi (Say-Hay-Key)

As you intone out loud, visualize each symbol going into the student's hand

Step 6 - Position: Kneel in Front of Student; Area Hands in Prayer, Hold with Left Hand over Heart

While still at student's front, place student's hands in prayer (Japanese call this gassho, pronounced gas-hoe) position and hold with your left hand.

Place your right hand over student's heart and then with your left hand, press student's hands against your right hand

First, visualize

 and intone out loud 3times Cho-Ku-Rei (Choh-Koo-Ray) Next, visualize

and intone out loud 3times HonSha-Ze-Sho-Nen (HonShaw-Zay-Show-Nen)
Lastly, visualize

and intone out loud 3times Sei-HeKi (Say-Hay-Key)

Step 7 – Finish by, criss-crossing the students hands over their heart and then criss-cross your hands on top of theirs; remain in this position until you feel that the process is completed (follow your intuition)

When finished, walk counter-clockwise to back of student, bow to Usui sensei and give a silent prayer of gratitude

(E.g. "*I give thanks of gratitude to the Reiki healing team for all assistance received during this attunement – thank you, thank-you, thank-you*")

While at the back of the student, draw

the Raku ∕ symbol to ground and seal the symbols into the student, plus disconnect your energy from the student's

Ring bell 1-time to signify completion (or advise student that attunement is completed)

Student bows first to Usui sensei, then to Reiki Master, leaves the room and returns to their chair to meditate

When all attunements are completed, change from attunement garment, do your cleansing exercise (E.g. dry brush or shower method) and wash hands (for sanitary purposes, plus to cleanse external energies)

Return to teaching room and with a guided meditation (see below), bring students back to the present time

Guided Meditation after Attunement

• You have now received attunement to Reiki level 2 and you will experience this in your own unique way

• You are feeling very relaxed and very peaceful

• Feel and know that the energy and power from the Reiki symbols are penetrating the very essence of your soul

• Feel and know that you are a very loving and powerful channel for the Reiki healing energy

• Feel and know that you are a powerful healing facilitator who will only perform Reiki for the highest good for self and others

• Know that your spirit healing team will assist you whenever you call upon their help and guidance

• Now I am going to count from 1 to 5 and when I reach number 5, you will return to the present time, take 3-deep breaths, open your eyes and you will feel very refreshed, plus invigorated

• 1...start to come back.....2.....you are slowing returning to conscious awareness.....3....4..... you are almost back......5....you are fully back in the present time.......take 3-deep breaths.....open your eyes......rub your fingers together......you are fully conscious and aware of the present

• If you feel unsteady or dizzy, take 3-deep breaths, drink some water or touch an inanimate object to help ground yourself

REIKI MASTER TEACHER LEVEL STEP-BY-STEP Of ATTUNEMENT PROCEDURE

Purpose of Attunement The main purpose of an attunement or **reiju** (pronounced Ray-joo) is to raise your energy level to re-connect you to your inner true self (soul), plus strengthen your connection to universal spiritual energy.

In Master Teacher Level, you are attuned to the Master empowerment symbol Dai-Ko-Myo, (pronounced Die-coe-me-oh) through one initiation.

 It activates the Master symbol enabling you to manifest your spiritual vision and compassion into the present time or into physical reality (into the "now"), so you can help others to empower themselves.

Preparing Students for Attunement Process (to relax student)

Play soft Reiki music

 Sit with feet flat on the floor, place hands on laps (avoid crossing limbs)
Close your eyes, take 3-deep breaths and relax
Take a moment to scan yourself

Starting at your feet and working upward toward your crown, observe any tenseness and relax each muscle

Say to students, "You are safe and secure at all times"

Procedure during Attunement

• Ring bell/gong 3times for student to enter attunement room

• When student enters the attunement room they will
• Bow to Reiki Master Teacher

• Bow to Usui sensei (to show respect)
• Sit on stool with back straight
• Feet flat on floor (legs are not crossed)
• Hands held loosely on lap (hands are not crossed)
• Close eyes and relax

Guided Meditation Script to Relax Students

• In front of you is a wide, staircase made of clear quartz crystal
• Walk over to the staircase until you are standing in front of it

• As I count from 1 to 10, I want you to climb the stairs until you reach the landing at the top

• 1 and 2 and 3 and 4 and 5 and 6 and 7 and 8 and 9 and 10

• You are now standing on the landing and in front of you is a white door

• Slowly walk over to the door & open it, then step over the threshold

• Remember, you are safe and secure at all times
• Before you is a beautiful, serene park, full of lush green trees and fragrant, colourful blooming flowers in all shape and sizes

• Their heady aroma permeates the air around you

• In front of you is a slide situated in front of a large pool filled with rainbow coloured water

• Walk over to the slide and as I count from 1 to 7, climb the stairs – 1 and 2 and 3 and 4 and 5 and 6 and 7

• Now sit down on the slide, don't worry about being fully dressed, just slide down into the water below

• Relax in the water, feel its invigorating, refreshing, crisp, coolness as it laps against your skin

• As you float and relax, be aware of what healing colour your body naturally absorbs

• Above you is the yellow glow of the afternoon sun, beating its warmth over you

• You feel so relaxed, so peaceful and very happy

• Stay in the water and enjoy yourself

• When you hear the bell ring three times, you will be ready to receive your attunement

• If it's your turn, slowly open your eyes, get up out of your chair and meet me at the door of the healing room

This attunes the student to the Master empowerment symbol Dai-Ko-Myo, (Die-coe-me-oh) through one initiation.

It activates the Master symbol enabling the student to manifest spiritual vision and compassion into the present time or into physical reality (into the "now"), so they can help others to empower themselves.

Step 1 - Position: Back of Student; Area – Shoulders and Crown

Stand behind the student and place your right hand on the student's shoulder. Connect your energy to the universal energy source by raising your left arm with hand facing upward (to receive universal energy) and visualize or draw the Master Symbol Dai-Ko-Myo (pronounced Die-

Coe-Me oh)  above the student's crown.

With your left arm still raised and left hand facing upward, place your right hand on top of student's crown and silently say a prayer or invocation.

 (E.g. *"I ask for universal blessings from spirit and the Reiki healing team to assist this student to become a compassionate, loving Reiki healer and teacher who will be filled with humility in order to serve humanity for the highest good"*)

Cup your hands, like a funnel, over student's crown, leaving a small opening for a blowing hole

Position your tongue (behind your upper teeth), take 3-deep belly breaths and contract your Hui-Yin.

Visualize white light entering your crown, travelling through your tongue, down the front of your body to the Hui Yin point (situated at Root Chakra or perineum), then back up your spine to the centre of your head (Fire Dragon energy)

Visualize

and intone silently 3times Dai-Ko-Myo (DieCoe-Me-oh) as you blow "Fire Dragon" energy into crown.

See the symbol penetrate into student's heart and travel along their arms into their hands; wait until you feel the process is completed before continuing.

Note: Release your Hui Yin after the blowing is completed

Step 2 - Position: Kneel in Front of Student; Area – Hands in Prayer, Sandwiched (little cup)

Walk counter-clockwise to student's front, place student's hands in prayer (called "**gassho**") position and then sandwich your hands over student's, in prayer position, with your finger tips touching each other like a pyramid (called little cup)

First, visualize

and intone silently 3times Dai-Ko-Myo (Die-Coe-Me-oh)

Next, visualize

and intone silently 3times Cho-Ku-Rei (Choh-Koo-Ray)

Next, visualize

and intone silently 3times
Hon-Sha-Ze-Sho-Nen
(Hon-Shaw-Zay-ShowNen)
Lastly,visualize

and intone silently 3times Sei-He-Ki (Say-HayKey)

Step 3 - Position: Kneel in Front of Student; Area Left
Hand on Heart

While still at student's front, place student's left hand over
their heart and have them keep it there while you
sandwich their right hand between yours (one above and
one below)

First, visualize

 symbol

going into the hand while intoning out loud 3times Dai-
KoMyo (Die-Coe-Me-oh)

Next, visualize

symbol going into the hand while intoning out loud 3times
Cho-KuRei (Choh-Koo-Ray)

Thirdly, visualize

symbol going into the hand while intoning out loud 3times
Hon-Sha-ZeSho-Nen (Hon-Shaw-Zay Show-Nen)
Lastly, visualize

symbol going into the hand while intoning out loud 3times
Sei-He-Ki (Say-Hay Key)

Step 4 - Position: Kneel in Front of Student; Area Hands
in Prayer, Hold with Left Hand over Heart

While still at student's front, place student's hands in
prayer (Japanese call this gassho, pronounced gas-hoe)
position and hold with your left hand; place your right
hand over student's heart.

Then with your left hand press student's hands (still in
prayer position) against your right hand

First, visualize

and intone out loud 3times Dai-Ko-Myo (Die-Coe-Me-oh)

Next, visualize

and intone out loud 3times ChoKu-Rei (Choh-KooRay)

Thirdly, visualize

and intone out loud 3times Hon-Sha-Ze-ShoNen (Hon-Shaw-ZayShow-Nen)

Lastly, visualize

and intone out loud 3times Sei-HeKi (Say-Hay-Key)

Step 5 - Position: Kneel in Front of Student; Area Right Hand on Heart

While still at student's front, place student's right hand over their heart and have them hold it there.

Then sandwich student's left hand between yours (one above and one below)

First, visualize

symbol going into the hand while intoning out loud 3times Dai-Ko-Myo (Die-Coe-Me-Oh) Next, visualize

symbol going into the hand while intoning loud 3times

Cho-Ku-Rei (Choh-Koo-Ray) Thirdly, visualize

symbol going into the hand while intoning out loud 3times Hon-Sha-Ze-Sho-Nen (Hon-Shaw-Zay-Show-Nen)

Lastly, visualize

symbol going into the hand while intoning out loud 3times Sei-He-Ki (Say-HayKey)

Step 6 - Position: Kneel in Front of Student; Area Hands in Prayer, Hold with Left Hand over Heart

While still at student's front, place student's hands in prayer (Japanese call this gassho, pronounced gas-hoe) position and hold with your left hand.

Place your right hand over student's heart and then with your left hand, press student's hands against your right hand

First, visualize

and intone out loud 3times Dai-Ko-Myo (Die-Coe-Me-oh) Next,

visualize

and intone out loud 3times Cho-Ku-Rei (Choh-Koo-Ray)

Thirdly, visualize

and intone out loud 3times Hon-Sha-Ze-ShoNen (Hon-Shaw-ZayShow-Nen)

Lastly, visualize

and intone out loud 3times Sei-He-Ki (Say-HayKey)

Step 7 – Finish by, criss crossing student's hands over their heart and then criss-cross your hands on top of theirs; remain in this position until you feel that the process is completed (follow your intuition)

Walk counter-clockwise to back of student, bow to Usui sensei and silently say a prayer of gratitude

(E.g. "*I give thanks of gratitude to the Reiki healing team for all assistance received during this attunement – thank-you, thank you, thank-you*")

While at the back of the student,

draw Raku ∤ symbol to ground and seal the symbols into the student, plus disconnect your energy from that of the student's. Visualize your energies being separated.

Ring bell 1-time to signify completion (or verbally advise student that attunement is completed)

Student bows first to Usui sensei, then to Reiki Master, leaves the room and returns to their chair to meditate

When all attunements are completed, change from attunement garment, do your cleansing exercise (E.g. dry brush or shower method) and wash hands (for sanitary purposes, plus to cleanse external energies)

Return to teaching room and with a guided meditation (see following, page), bring students back to the present

Guided Meditation after Attunement

• You have now received attunement to Reiki Master Teacher level and you will experience this in your own unique way

• You are feeling very relaxed and very peaceful

• Feel and know that the energy and power from the Reiki symbols are penetrating the very essence of your soul

• Feel and know that you are a very loving and powerful channel for the Reiki healing energy

• Feel and know that you are a powerful healing facilitator who will only perform Reiki for the highest good for self and others.

• Feel and know that you will become a trusting and dedicated teacher who will instill high moral ethics in your students, as well as compassion and love

• Know that your spirit healing team will assist you whenever you call upon their help and guidance

• Now I am going to count from 1 to 5 and when I reach number 5, you will return to the present time, take 3-deep breaths, open your eyes and you will feel very refreshed, plus invigorated

• 1...start to come back.....2.....you are slowing returning to conscious awareness.....3....4..... you are almost back......5....you are fully back in the present time.......take 3-deep breaths.....open your eyes......rub your fingers together......you are fully conscious and aware of the present

• If you feel unsteady or dizzy, take 3-deep breaths, drink some water or touch an inanimate object to help ground yourself

Archangels & Reiki

The term "Archangel" means "An Angel of Higher kind."

The Archangels take care of people by strengthening and assisting them in every walk of life.

They do not believe in any particular religion, caste or creed, and help us to heal or get healed if they are called upon with a pure heart.

But it is very important to keep in mind that they do not interfere in our Karma.
There are Four Primary Archangels associated with the four main Usui Symbols.

The Archangel are Michael, Gabriel, Rafael and Uriel.

Michael– "Who is Like a God"

He is in charge of protection, justice, and truth. Michael grants miracles and gets rid of toxins, lower energies and releases spirit.

Michael is associated with the Dai Ko Myo

He also oversees a healer's life purpose.
You can summon Michael if you find yourself under psychic attack or when your job is too demanding with impossible deadlines to reach and people to handle.

Gabriel – "Messenger of God"

Gabriel is the only female Archangel in charge of
communication.
Contact Gabriel If your third eye is closed.
If you want a child, she may help you conceive or bring
news of conception.

Gabriel representing Cho Ku Rei helps you to stay on life
path and know soul's plan.
Gabriel helps raped women
She resembles white and purple light.

Raphael – "God heals"

Raphael is an archangel that takes great interest in helping those who ask.
He helps us to be better healers.
Raphael grants love, miracles and grace.

Raphael representing Sei Hei Ki He is the most friendly and jovial of all Angels, and is sweet and loving.
His color is green light.

Call upon Raphael when you are traveling.
Raphael does not only help you to heal from physical, emotional and mental pain but also heals wounds from past lives & childhood trauma.
Raphael helps to find lost pets and even lost soulmate.
He can help in marriages.

Uriel – "The Light of God"

Uriel is the wisest Archangel because of his intellectual information and geniusness in problem solving.
He is very subtle and he answers prayers in sudden brilliant ways.

Uriel represents Hon Sha Ze Sho Nen

Uriel heals all natural calamities and the Earth.
He is an angel of Transformation & Transmutation.
Call on him to release the painful burdens and memories of the past.

His color is golden light.

Setting & Fulfilling Intentions With Reiki and Archangel Michael

When we desire something, the first thing we need to do is set an intention.

Often, our intentions are not strong enough.
When this is the case, we end up sending mixed signals to the Universe.

It is no wonder then that desires that are not backed by strongintentions take longer to manifest.
We will have to struggle and stress ourselves a lot more when our intentions are not strong and clear.

One of the primary reasons for the inability to set clear intentions is that we often feel undeserving of what we desire.

Many of us are conditioned to believe that life involves plenty of sacrifice and hardship and that an amazing life is the privilege of a chosen few.

This is a self limiting belief that can make life boring and hard.

The first thing we need to be aware of is that everyone deserves to have a good life.

No matter how a person appears on the surface, deep down he carries the same light in him as the one carried by a Saint or other Higher Being.

Every single soul is a child of the Universe.
People make mistakes, go through hardships and face challenges in order to learn life lessons and balance karmas.

However, no one is less deserving because of who he is or what he might have done in the past.

So, before you set an intention, it is crucial that you first change any self limiting beliefs you may have about your right to deserve.

To aid This shift, we can use written affirmations.

Start by writing a page of the following affirmations in a journal every day.
You can either write all of them or choose one that you resonate most with.

1. *I am a child of the Universe. I deserve to enjoy all the good that life has to offer.*

2. *I deserve to have all of my heartfelt desires fulfilled.*

3. *I open my arms to receive all that I have asked for. I truly deserve it.*

After writing a page of this affirmation, draw the Reiki symbols Hon Sha Ze Sho Nen, Sei Hei Ki and Cho Ku Rei anywhere on the page.

You can draw as many as you feel like.
Give Reiki to the page.

This will help strengthen your new positive belief and also heal any feelings of not deserving that may be buried deep in your subconscious.

You could also write or say the following prayer to connect with Archangel Michael and take his assistance to heal self---limiting beliefs.

"Dear Archangel Michael, Please help me feel the truth of my own divine light. Please help me
to see that I am a child of the Universe and that I deserve to have all my desires fulfilled.
I request you to clear and heal all the self---limiting beliefs that I carry in my subconscious. Thank you."

Once you are clear about the fact that you deserve and have absorbed this new positive belief, start working on your intentions.

Keep these pointers in mind as you work on your intentions.

1. Writing is extremely powerful when it comes to intentions.

Write your intention down in a journal.
Write it in the present tense.

Draw the Reiki symbols on the page and give Reiki to it once every day.

2. Visualise how you would feel or what you would be doing if the intention has already manifested.

For example, if your intention is to conceive and give birth to a child, visualize how it would feel to be carrying that baby and also to hold him or her in your arms after the birth.

Visualise the details of the pregnancy and birth and make everything extremely positive.
Feel it like it is happening now.

3. If you feel any discomfort or fear as you set your intentions, call upon Archangel Michael for help.

Talk to him and express your fears.

His warrior like energies will help heal any blocks that you may be holding with respect to fulfilling your desires.

If you are unable to pinpoint the exact fear, call upon Archangel Michael just before falling asleep.

Ask him to work on your fears and blocks as you sleep.

When we are asleep, our rational mind is at rest and we are naturally more open to healing.

Do this every night until you feel extremely comfortable with your intentions.

4. Once your intentions are set, do not worry about how they will manifest.

Take any action that you need to in order to manifest your intention and then let go.

Remember your intentions have been charged with Reiki. Reiki is an intelligent energy and we do not have to instruct it on how it should go about fulfilling our desires.

It knows exactly how to manifest our desires and also the timing in which to manifest them.

Set the intention, give positive energy to it every day and then let it go.

If you begin to feel anxious about the manifestation, call upon Archangel Michael again and request him to help you let go.

Strong intentions produce clear results.
ALWAYS! And with the loving unconditional support of Reiki and Archangel Michael, you will be well on your way towards living your desire

Healing Fear with Reiki & Archangel Michael

What is your greatest fear?

What makes your heart beat fast, your hands sweaty and your mind spin?

What triggers your anxiety?

Almost everyone has at least a couple of fears.

Some fears are small, while others are big and strong. The strong fears are infused with a power so great that they overpower even the strongest and sanest of folks.

A person who is normally composed can turn into a nervous wreck when in the grip of fear.

Rationality and logic vanish and no amount of reassurance from people helps.

As a child, my greatest fear was that I would lose my mother.

I had an irrational and almost obsessive fear of losing her. It was so strong that I would cry in fear if she travelled without me or left me alone with other family, especially at night.

This fear of losing a loved one is quite common among people.

Some other common fears include:
- Fear of death
- Fear of illness
- Fear of being harmed
- Fear of darkness
- Fear of travelling
- Fear of failure
- Fear of ghosts
- Fear of abandonment
- Fear of flying

This list is practically endless.
If you ask everyone you know about their fears, you will come across a variety of fears, some of which you can't even connect with!

But that is the nature of fear. It is most often irrational and imaginary.

This is different from the kind of fear you feel when faced with a truly dangerous situation.
However, being in dangerous situations is certainly not an everyday occurrence.

This kind of logical thinking does not stop us from being fearful!

So, how can we help ourselves when we stand face to face with our fears?

Here is a technique that can help you when you find yourself in the grip of irrational fear

- Sit or lie down comfortably.
- Close your eyes and take a few deep breaths.
- Feel your fear in all its intensity.

Do not be afraid of feeling the fear.
For instance, if you are afraid of an illness, feel the fear and all the scary details your mind projects about this illness.

Don't worry, this will not manifest the illness.
Since the intention behind feeling the fear is to release the energy associated with it, know that you are safe.

• Now bring your awareness to your body.
In which part of your body do you feel the effects of this fear?

Do you feel tightness in your solar plexus or chest?

Or do you feel heaviness in your head?

• Once you locate the part of the body in which the fear manifests, place one of your palms on that part.

• Give a shape and colour to this fear.
Go with the first image that comes to your mind.
Do not analyze.

View this image in your mind's eye.
• Now stretch your other hand, with the palm facing up.

Request Archangel Michael or any other Spirit Guide you are comfortable working with to place their palm in yours.

• Feel the powerful energy emanating from this fearless being.
Breathe in and absorb some of his energies.

• Now feel the power of your own being.
You are inherently powerful.

The scary voice in your head that makes you feel weak and fearful is the voice of the Ego.

• With this awareness of your power, see yourself blowing the symbols Hon Sha Ze Sho Nen, Sei Hei Ki and Cho Ku Rei to the image of the fear you hold in your mind's eye.

Third level practitioners can also use the Master Symbol.

• See the symbols flying towards the image of the fear and attaching themselves to it.

See the fear being enveloped in Reiki and being transmuted into power and love.

• Do this for as long as you feel like.
If you feel weak or powerless while in the midst of the process, remind yourself that Archangel Michael (or your Spirit Guide) is with you.

What is there to fear when you are in the company of such powerful beings?

They are there to assist you and help you recognize your own power.
So, take their help.

• Once you feel peaceful, thank Reiki and Archangel Michael (or your Spirit Guide) for their assistance.

Do this process whenever you find yourself in the grip of irrational fear.

It may need to be done several times, often over months, before the fear is healed fully.

You may also receive intuitive messages about other steps you can take to help with the healing.

Cord cutting is particularly useful to heal deep rooted fears.

If the fear overwhelms you to such an extent that you cannot even lie still and relax to do this process, it would be wise to work with a competent Reiki Master.

Once the fear is at least partially healed and you feel comfortable, you can start working independently.

Your fears can be healed.

You are much more powerful than any fearful projection of your Ego.

You just have forgotten how powerful you are and it is now time for you to remember it!

Build Your Healing Practice with Archangel Michael

Are you aware of your life's purpose?
What is your calling?

What special gifts do you have that you can share with the world?

If You are a Reiki practitioner, Reiki is something you may wish to share with the world.

Are you doing justice to your Reiki practice and to all your other gifts?
If not, what is holding you back?

Several healers feel a calling from the depths of their heart.

They can vaguely remember what they came here to do.

They are aware that they have innate healing abilities with which they can make a difference.

However, they feel stuck on their path.
Does that sound like you?

That was me too, some years ago ☺ Right through my college days and a subsequent six years in another career, something didn't feel right about what I was doing with my life.

I had a hard time figuring out what that "something" was.

All I knew was that I was not happy with the academic courses I did or the jobs I worked at.

People thought I was an idealist on the lookout for a perfect career.
But I knew deep down that I was not looking for an ideal set up.

I knew I had a different purpose to fulfil and it just took time for me to figure out what that purpose was.

The purpose was actually unfolding all along.
All the experiences I had and the challenges I faced before and even after I became a Reiki practitioner helped me reach where I am today.
Being determined about my life's path and not being swayed by others' opinions helped immensely.

The good news is that you can do it too!
You can follow your heart and fulfil your purpose.

You can use your healing abilities and teach others about it too.

You can create a life that feels meaningful to you and which satisfies the longing of your soul.
All you need is a strong will and a bit of courage.

Take Small Steps Each Day

If you wish to have an independent Reiki or spiritual teaching practice, start moving in the direction of your dreams today.

Maybe you can't afford to quit your current job and set up a full time Reiki practice right away.
But you can certainly accomplish a little bit each day.

If you wish to do more healing work and you don't have clients and students yet, heal with Reiki in other ways.

You may have a garden at home.
Why not give Reiki to your plants?
If you have pets at home, why not pamper them with Reiki treatments?
Give Reiki to Planet Earth and play a role in its healing.

And most important of all, heal yourself with Reiki every day.
Remember, the more you heal yourself, the more you are able to help others heal.

These may seem like small steps but they can go a long way in helping you to fulfil your life's purpose.

With every small step you take, you inspire the Universe to take ten steps more.
And you soon find yourself living life at your highest potential.

Call on Archangel Michael

You can also call on Archangel Michael to help you move ahead on your life's path.
Michael loves to help healers and spiritual teachers fulfil their purpose.

The best way to connect with Michael is to have a personal interaction with him.
This is one technique you may want to try:

1. Go outdoors in nature (preferably in your own private garden or roof terrace).

If that is not feasible, don't worry.
You can do it indoors too.

2. Take a few deep breaths and relax.
Call upon Archangel Michael and request him to be by your side.

Call him from your heart.

3. When you call on Michael, you can be certain that he will be there.

You may feel a warm presence beside you or you may just sense that he is by your side.

Once you intuitively sense that Michael is beside you, hold his hand.

If you ask for your hand to be held, rest assured that it will be held (even if you can't feel it).
Or you may find that Michael puts his arm around you.

Trust your intuition and go with the flow.
Stroll around your garden with him.

Walking with Archangel Michael is like walking with a wise old friend and sharing your life's story with him along the way!

4. Pour your heart out to Michael.
Talk to him loudly (if possible), as it can help you connect better.

No one is around to judge you or laugh at you.
Tell him about your desires and aspirations with regards to your life's purpose.

Tell him about your fears and about everything that is holding you back.
Ask him to guide you.

5. Notice all the empowering thoughts and feelings that enter your awareness as you walk.

These are Michael's messages for you.
If you receive a message that does not feel right, know that it is coming from the Ego and not from Michael.

The angels always give us empowering messages, even when the messages have challenging guidance.

Trust your intuition and accept only those messages that feel right.

6. Thank the Archangel for his guidance and request him to continue helping you with your life's purpose.

Just the act of walking with Archangel Michael will help you feel powerful.

It can help you develop a strong will and to become your own Master and guide.

His messages serve as additional guidance.
There is no better time to start than now.

Do whatever you can to fulfil your life's purpose today, no matter how small the step.

And allow Archangel Michael to be your mentor.
Do you know how blessed we are to have angelic guides and mentors? ☺

Be fearless and know that you can accomplish your life's purpose.

You can be an amazing Reiki healer, a powerful spiritual teacher and everything else that will make a difference to you and to the world!

Guided Meditation to Connect with Archangel Raphael

Archangel Raphael is known as the supreme angel of healing.

He reaches across numerous religions and belief systems just as the healing art of Reiki does.

He loves to be called upon and welcomes any opportunity to show you a sign of his presence.
Raphael's greatest joy is to bring healing to your life.

He has a special affinity for those who feel the calling to work as healers.

He will watch over you and use you as a vessel to help others.
He emits a beautiful green emerald healing light.

I first came in contact with Archangel Raphael during a meditation session.

I knew that I loved the world of Reiki and that my calling was to help others heal.

I wasn't sure however if Reiki was something I should pursue as a business or if it was just a hobby.

Raphael appeared to me in my meditation and said that I was to move forward and be a healer.
He promised to look over me and help me be a vessel to bring healing to many around me.

He instantly alleviated any worries I had and helped give me confidence in the direction I was to go.

Before each Reiki session I have with a client I ask him to please help heal the client for their greatest good.

He has brought so much peace to my life and inspired my business name of Divine Light Therapies.

One of the things that I love the most about Archangel Raphael is that he is so easy to make contact with.

He loves to show you his presence and receives a great deal of joy from making a connection with you.

Raphael can help bring so much love and healing to your life as well as being able to show you how to bring it to others.

Here is a very simple guided meditation routine of how to easily connect with Archangel Raphael.

1. Pick a **place** where it is quiet and you are most at peace.
This can be an outdoor space or indoor space.

2. Reiki the room or space with whatever **symbols** you feel called to use.
I like to use the Master symbol but any symbols you feel called to use will be correct for you.

3. Next, if you prefer to mediate with **music** put music on.
Music can really help some people to clear their mind and have a better connection.

4. Next, light a **candle**.
I like to use white or pink but many people find it easier to connect by using a green candle since that is the color that radiates from Raphael.

5. Sit in your prepared meditative space and close your eyes.

Spend a minute slowly breathing in and out, in and out, in and out.
At this point picture Raphael coming to you and standing before you.

Open up to whatever **messages** you feel he is trying to tell you.

6. If you have any **questions** for him now is the time to ask! Pay attention to whatever thoughts you suddenly have.

These thoughts could be your answer! Do not dismiss any information you are receiving.

If it doesn't make sense right away it may make sense to you a few days or weeks later.

7. After ten minutes of being in this meditative state (or however long you feel called to stay) picture a **majestic green light** filling your space.

This light is clearing your space of anything that is bothering you and is bringing healing energy to you.

8. **Thank** Raphael for his loving presence and then open your eyes feeling relaxed and at peace.

9. At this point you may like to write down any **messages or symbols** you feel you were given so you can refer back to them later.

Wishing you all love and light!

Communication with Departed Loved Ones: Reiki & Archangel Azrael

Archangel Azrael is known as "The Angel of Death."

He helps souls cross over comfortably to the other side.

He also helps these souls communicate with near and dear ones on Earth.

People who are alive can also take his assistance to establish communication with the souls of their departed loved ones.

As Reiki practitioners, we have the added benefit of using Reiki along with help from Archangel Azrael.

Reiki energy being soft and loving creates a safe and peaceful space for soul communication to happen.

This kind of communication should only be done only to express such things that would help us and also help the souls of our loved ones.

Positive and kind words that were unexpressed when the person was alive can certainly be expressed.

Asking for forgiveness for any pain we caused them and sending our love is also perfectly fine.

In short, any message that comes from the heart is good. Love is the key.

If what you wish to convey is not coming from a place of love (that is, it is coming from the Ego), don't express it.

Your intuition will guide you.

Here is a brief outline of the process:

• Keep a piece of paper and pen with you.

• Sit in a quiet place where you will be left undisturbed.

• You can play soothing music and also light a candle if it helps.

• Take a few deep breaths and get into a meditative state.

• Visualise the room being flooded with Reiki.
You can also draw any symbols that you are guided to in the air.

• Bring your awareness to your heart.
You can place your palm on the heart to connect with it.

What message of love does your heart wish to send to the soul of your loved one?

Start writing the message on the piece of paper.
Keep your words positive and loving.

• Give Reiki to this piece of paper.
This will strengthen the element of love in your message.

• Call upon Archangel Azrael.
If you work angel card decks, pick any card of Archangel Azrael from the deck to connect with him.

If you wish to, you can also place the card along with your piece of paper.
Request him to take this message to your loved one.

• You can also request Azrael to bring a message back to you from your loved one.

• Express your gratitude to the Archangel for his assistance.

• Put the piece of paper away in a safe place.

• Thereafter, notice any messages you may receive from the other side.

These messages may come in the form of feelings you may feel a deep sense of peace or you may feel a surge of love.

Unhealed feelings that you may have carried about your past relationship with this person are suddenly healed.

You may also receive messages in the form of words that you read somewhere or as songs that play on the radio or television.

It may also be in the form of visits from certain animals or birds.

Each one's experience is unique.
You will know it is a message for you when you receive it.

• Do not analyze the message by allowing your logical mind to kick in.
Trust your feelings and accept the message you get.

• Once you have received your message, discard the paper by either burning or burying it.

This technique is particularly useful when we wish to express love and forgiveness to our departed loved ones.

When people are alive, we sometimes take them for granted.

We may also focus only on the negative aspects of their personality.

And when the person is no more, we realize their value and also recognize their positive traits.

This tends to bring up feelings of sadness and guilt in us.

However, feeling sad or guilty does not help anyone.

As we grow spiritually, it is important to remind ourselves constantly that the core of our being is pure love.

Anything that is not love is not who we are.
Due to our identification with the ego, all of us err from time to time.

So, if you feel sad or guilty about something you did or did not do (or something you said or did not say) when a loved one was with you, it is not too late.

It is possible to express your feelings even now.
Rest assured that the power of love would heal everything that is unhealed in all of space and time and restore the flow of love in your relationship.

Chakra Clearing with Reiki and Archangel Metatron

I do Angel Card Readings every single day to receive guidance for my personal growth.

For a period in time, I kept drawing the card of Archangel Metatron.

This card asked me to clear my chakras with his help.

I did not take this guidance seriously and kept putting off working with Archangel Metatron for several days.

But like all card readers would know, you keep drawing the same cards until you follow the guidance being given to you.

I drew the card so many times that I finally decided to work with this mighty Archangel.

Archangel Metatron heals with sacred geometric shapes and uses a tool that some refer to as a "*Metatron Cube*".

In order to facilitate healing, he passes his cube right through your energy body.

The cube rotates as it moves through your energy field and clears toxins from each of your chakras.

When I finally used the Metatron cube to heal myself, I found the results to be quite amazing.
I could feel the cube clearing away all toxic energies as it rotated.

Since then I have begun to take the assistance of Archangel Metatron and his sacred cube during some Reiki healing that I know would benefit from this additional help.

If you have pressing issues with any of your chakras or would just like a thorough cleansing of all your chakras, you will benefit from working with Archangel Metatron as well.

This technique can be easily incorporated with your daily routine of Reiki self-healing.

You will not need to use this technique every day.

You can use it once every few days depending on the health of your chakras.
Trust your intuition and use it when you feel like.

Here is how you go about it:

1. Take a deep breath.

2. Call upon Archangel Metatron to assist you with clearing your chakras.

If you work with angel cards and have the Archangel Metatron card with you, you can place it close to you during the healing.

3. Visualise the Archangel and his cube.
Do not worry too much about the visual details.
Your intention to connect with the Archangel and his cube will ensure that you are connected.

4. Visualise the Archangel sending his cube towards the top of your head.
Visualise the cube spinning inside your crown chakra.

Intuitively scan the chakra for traces of toxins.
Feel these toxins being cleared by the spinning cube.

5. Next move to the third eye chakra and repeat the same process.

Similarly, move the cube through each of the chakras and allow it to work on each one, thereby clearing every chakra of toxic debris.

6. Trust your intuition.
Let the cube move as it wishes to.

There is no strict rule to be followed as to which chakra
must be cleared first.

You may find the cube moving randomly from chakra to
chakra and also moving back to do more work on chakras
that were already cleared.
Do not analyze.

Just go with the flow and relax.
You will not make a mistake when you trust your intuition.

7. Once you feel that you are done, thank the Archangel
for his assistance with this healing.

8. Proceed to do a full body Reiki healing as usual.

9. Drink plenty of water.
There is no limit to the number of ways in which we can
heal ourselves.

It is always nice to experiment with different techniques
and absorb the benefit that each technique has to offer.

The beauty of Reiki lies in its flexibility.
It can be incorporated with most other techniques and it
works so beautifully.

If you like healing with the angels, you are sure to enjoy
working with Archangel Metatron and his sacred cube!

Reiki and Archangel Haniel

Archangel Haniel has a lovely energy that resonates with
the moon.

The crystal associated with her is moonstone.
She can help us when we feel sensitive and out of
balance.

Working with her may be particularly helpful to women who find themselves going off balance at varied times of the menstrual cycle.

If you are a woman and you face this problem every month, you can connect with Archangel Haniel.

Haniel's soft energy can ease hormonal fluctuations and help you maintain a state of harmony and balance.

This apart, she also helps anyone who feels sensitive, unworthy/unlovable and out of balance in general (men included).

The best time to work with Archangel Haniel is during the time of the full moon.
But you don't have to wait for the full moon to connect with her.

You can also call on her at other times and she will be happy to help you. Using or wearing a moonstone crystal can help you connect with her energies better.

Healing with Reiki and Moonstone

• Ensure your moonstone crystal has been cleaned and cleared of all negative energies.

• Hold the crystal between your palms and charge it with Reiki for a while.

• Call upon Archangel Haniel and ask her to bless this stone with her energy.

• Request Archangel Haniel to sit beside you as you prepare to heal yourself with Reiki.

• Begin to do a full body Reiki healing.

• As you heal yourself, place the moonstone crystal on whatever chakra or part of the body that you are guided to.
Trust your intuition and feel free to move it around.

You will not make a mistake when you trust your feelings.

• You can also request Archangel Haniel to heal you with her energies and just relax as the energies work on you. This act of receiving from Haniel will help you understand that it is OK to receive in life.

A lot of energetic imbalances occur when we become perpetual givers and also when we try to be in control at all times.

We must also learn to receive and to let go of control at times.

This helps our energies stay in harmony and balance.

Full Moon Healing with Archangel Haniel

• Go outdoors on the evening of the full moon.
Your own garden, balcony or roof terrace would work
best.

If that is not feasible, you can do it indoors in a space that
offers you a view of the full moon.

• Take a few deep breaths to relax and center yourself.

• Call on Archangel Haniel.
Say,
*"Dear Archangel Haniel, Please be with me now and help
me heal."*

• Look at the full moon and visualize Archangel Haniel
standing behind it.

• Intend that the energies from Haniel and the moon wash
over you from head to toe and bring balance to your
body, mind and spirit.

• Bask in this energy for as long as you like.

• Once done, thank Haniel and the moon for their help.

• Drink plenty of water.
This meditation can also be done when the full moon is
not around.

All you need to do is visualize a full moon and proceed to
heal yourself as described above.
Enjoy feeling balanced and harmonious!

Live Your Passions & Create a Colourful Life with Reiki & Archangel Haniel

What are you passionate about in life?
How many of your passions are you living?
Are you aware of your passions?

I would like to share my list of passions.
I am passionate about:
1. Life
2. Music
3. Dance
4. Healing
5. Energy work
6. Teaching others about healing, energy work and angels
7. Angel card readings
8. Reading
9. Writing
10. Nurturing my child
11. Romance and love
12. Good food
13. Travel
14. Rest & Relaxation
15. Spiritual Growth and learning
16. Nature
17. Pampering myself and my inner child
18. Spending time by myself

Exercise

Before you read further, take a pen and paper and make a list of all the things that you are passionate about.

We may add more things to the list as life goes by.

Passion does not always involve "big" stuff.
You can even be passionate about relishing a cup of tea.

It is perfectly normal to be passionate about the small things in life.

Ultimately, it is those small things that determine the quality of our lives on a day-to-day basis.

Now look at the list of passions that you have made.

Spend some time reflecting on all that you have written.

How many of your passions are you living?
Are you satisfied with what you see?

Or would you like to add more colour to your life by living your passions on a day-to-day basis?

It takes **courage** to live your passions because it often involves being criticized or misunderstood by family and friends.

Everyone does not understand our passions and may not be fully supportive of us living our passions.

But life is meant to be lived fully.
Every day can be so full of joy and meaning, if only we could allow our passions to lead us.

So, the first thing to do is to decide that you will dedicate at least some time everyday to living at least one of your passions.

If your family is supportive of this, good for you!
If not, you will need to have a heart to heart conversation
with them and explain why this is important to you.

Most people understand when something is communicated
to them respectfully.

For instance, you may feel the need to spend some time
alone everyday to just be by yourself.

If you have never expressed this need of yours in the
past, it may come as a surprise to those closest to you.

Nevertheless, if it is on your list of passions, you will
benefit if you give yourself that time alone every day.

When you give yourself the permission to do this, it
means you love yourself and like to take care of yourself.

And when you take good care of yourself, you also end
up taking good care of the people close to you.

The following pointers can guide you as you work on living
your passions and making your life more meaningful.

Make the Time

Allocate time slots in your weekly schedule to live your
passions it could be an hour every day, a few hours every
week or one day in a week, as per your convenience.

It would be ideal if you could devote some time to at least
a couple of your passions every day.

But if that is not possible, make sure you at least dedicate
one day a week to living your passions.

Chart/Vision Board

Collect pictures that reflect your passions from
newspapers and magazines.

Stick all the pictures on a chart or board and hang the chart in a place where it is easily visible to you during the course of the day.

You can even draw the Reiki symbols on the chart if you wish to.

Looking at this chart will inspire you to live your passions!

Reiki & Archangel Haniel

Give Reiki to your list of passions and to your chart whenever possible.

This will add energy to your passions and make them a lot more powerful.

You can also take the help of Archangel Haniel to live your passions, especially when you need to take risks to do so.

For example, someone who is initially passionate about an activity may, over time, feel a strong calling to convert this passion into a full time career.

When this happens, the person may have to take certain risks and move past comfort zones.

However, when something is felt as a true calling, it is meant to be part of our life's plan and purpose.

And we are sure to receive support from the Universe as we make life changes to accommodate our passions.

However, the only requirement is that we ask for help.

When you feel afraid or unsure about living a passion of yours or about moving past your comfort zone, call upon Archangel Haniel.

Haniel whose name means **"Glory of God"** can help you use your potential to the fullest and make your transition into the unknown comfortable.

When we were children, we were naturally tuned into our passions and naturally believed that life was a joyous experience meant to be lived passionately.

As we grew older, we were conditioned to believe that life is a struggle.

As a result, many of us developed the belief that having fun and living passionately is something meant only for the young.

Nothing could be further from the truth.

Age is just a number and has absolutely nothing to do with living your passions or having fun.
The spirit of the child that you once were is still alive in you.
All you need to do is recognize it and set it free.

Once you set it free, this child like presence in you will help you live all of your passions and make life a truly amazing journey!

Reiki Yourself and Your Children to Sleep with the Help of the Angels

I am a Reiki Master and have used Reiki for all sorts of things from healings, to room cleansings to protection, to charging things.
I have my own Reiki business and feel it is my calling in life.

But even with all of this it was in a moment of desperation, and burnout at the end of my day from being a single parent of two little girls that did not like bedtime that I came up with a way to easily put my children to sleep.

While laying in bed one night completely and utterly exhausted from 2 hours of bargaining, tears and deal making about bedtime with my children I thought to myself that there has got to be a better way to do bedtime.

Then it hit me like lightning.

Why had I not been using Reiki and all of the other work that I do?

I use it in every other area of my life.
Why not bedtime with my children?
At that moment I formed a new plan.

The method that I used uses a symbol that you must be attuned to a Reiki Master level to use.

However, I believe that use of the other symbols would have wonderful effects as well and get you to the same peaceful place.

I do call in the help of Angels here.

If you are a Reiki Practitioner but do not believe in angels you could just use the Reiki and color work alone.

My new routine is as follows:

1. I put my daughters in their bed and Reiki their room.

2. I put the Master Symbol on every wall, window, bed, ceiling, floor and door.

3. I create a ball of white light in my hand that I then visualize going up and expanding throughout the room removing all that is negative out.

4. I then begin a guided meditation where I call in the Angels.

I have a special connection with Archangel Raphael so that is the angel I start with but any will work for you.

I go through my mediation with each Angel standing around my children's bed throwing a color up into the room that clears the room, goes down through their body (starting at their head then working slowly down to their toes).

Then finally the light goes down into the ground taking all of their troubles away and then heals the Earth.

I go through the chakra colors here, one color after another.

5. I then end it with the Angles giving thanks for allowing them to bring these loving colors to the children and do one big master healing symbol in the center of the room.

The beauty of this routine is that you can make it as short or long as you like.
When I do it the session averages ten minutes and my kids are fast asleep by the end of the guided meditation.

These are children that normally fight bedtime.
They look forward to this routine and bedtime is no longer a struggle.
I use this routine on myself as well and it puts me in a deeply relaxed state.

Allowing Reiki and Angels to assist with bedtime with their Divine light has been one of my favorite experiences with using Reiki so far.

attention:
Remember, that the angel above is just an intermediary of god power.
All requests should be addressed to the Creator.
They are only divine messengers with medium your prayer

Additional Chapter Kundalini Reiki

Training Manual

Kundalini Reiki

Reiki Master: Yan Nurindra

Introduction

Training Target

- The participant can channel Reiki energy.
- The participant can perform self-healing and other-healing.
- The participant understand the use of programs available in Kundalini Reiki tradition.
- The participant can provide attunement to others.

Training Rules

- The participants shall silent their cellphone, pager or any device that has the potential to cause noise that can interfere with the course of training.
- The participants are requested to temporarily put all large metals/leather accessories (glasses, wallets, belts, etc.) during Attunement, considering that the equipment can refract energy during the attunement.

Attention

- Reiki is a Supplementary Treatment, and is not intended to replace "Medical Healing". Reiki practitioners are not allowed to advice patients to stop the healing process from the doctor.
- Reiki practitioners are not allowed to diagnose the disease, unless the relevant Reiki practitioners are competent medical experts (for example, a doctor).

Post-Attunement Effect

After a person has attained an Attunement for the first time, the person may experience several possible effects of Post-Attunement, where these effects are normal and nothing to worry about. The effects are as follows:

- Over energy

  The etheric energy flows continuously, circulating throughout the etheric body tissue.

- Detoxification

  There is an increase in the frequency of defecation and urination.

- Over heating

  Body temperature tends to increase.

- Changes in Sleep Pattern

  The patient is more likely to feel sleepy.

The effects above are only temporary, because there is an attunement of internal "chi" flow and these effects are positive (not due to diseases).

Basic Principles of Reiki and Etheric Healing

Ki and Reiki

Holistic Healing Theory

To live a healthy life, humans do not only need sufficient foods and drinks, but also need "Ki". Disruption in the "Ki" circulation will cause disruption in the "etheric body" followed by a sickness phenomenon in the physical body.

Holistic healing works in the etheric body layer which will indirectly affect the physical body.

The Universal Life Force Energy

The universal life force energy is called differently in various countries, including Chi, Ki, Mana, Prana, and Barraka.

In the Japanese exoteric system, there are 7 levels of Ki or the life force energy, namely Kekki, Shioke, Mizuke, Kuki, Denki, Jiki, and Reiki (from the highest to lowest levels).

Reiki-Ho

Reiki-Ho is an esoteric system that can utilize Reiki energy optimally for various purposes, including self-healing and other-healing.

Reiki-Ho was discovered in 1923 by Sensei Mikao Usui, after meditating for a while at Mount Kurama, Japan.

The History of Spreading Reiki Around The World

In April 1922, Sensei Mikao Usui moved to Tokyo and started the first Reiki-Ho organization named Usui Reiki Ryoho Gakkai.

In the following years, he initiated Chijiro Hayashi as a teacher, then he initiated Hawayo Takata, a woman who has spread Reiki to the South American regions.

This process continued to other 22 people who then became Western Reiki Masters. Starting from 1980, Reiki has spread to 5 Continents.

Traditional Reiki

Vajra Reiki

Rainbow Reiki

Usui-Tibetan Reiki

Tera-Mai Reiki

Seichim Reiki

Tummo Reiki

Prema Reiki

Golden Reiki

New Reiki

Reiki was developed by Reiki Masters, who then found the other exoteric techniques according to traditional Reiki, including Tao, Johrei, Tibetan, etc.

The new exoteric techniques in Reiki were found based on Reiki Master's interpretation, channeling, local community tradition or culture, and experiment.

The techniques are:

Sacred Path Reiki

Quantum Reiki

Tibetan Soul Star Reiki

Tibetan Reiki

Radiant Technique Reiki

Neo Zen Reiki

Karuna Reiki

Raku Kai Reiki

Johrei Reiki

Etc.

Energy Lineage

1. Kuthumi

Kuthumi is an ascended Reiki Master, a master known physically had lived in India and Tibet in the 19th century and last known as a spiritual teacher in Kashmir, India. At this time, Kuthumi's teaching can be obtained through channeling group activities led by Madame Blavatsky, the founder of The Theosophical Society.

2. Ole Gabrielsen

Ole Gabrielsen was a Meditation and Kundalini Grandmaster from Denmark who had long channeled Kunthumi, and finally received Kundalini Reiki initiation from Kuthumi.

3. Yan Nurindra

4. Kundalini Reiki Practitioners

Basic Characteristics of Kundalini Reiki

- Kundalini Reiki does not require physical Attunement.
- It is specially designed to awaken Kundalini and raise Kundalini Fire.
- Its use is easy and simple (program)
- It does not require the symbols.
- It can be combined with techniques from other traditions.
- The attunement procedures are easy and simple.
- Practitioners will receive several different energies.

Energy

- Reiki
- Kundalini Reiki
- Diamond Reiki
- Gold Reiki (optional)

Steps of Attunement

Before Attunement

After Kundalini Reiki -1

Chakra: Crown, Heart, Palm

After Kundalini Reiki -2

Chakra: Ajina, Kundalini Awakening, raise the Fire at least to the Navel Chakra

After Kundalini Reiki –3

Chakra: Throat, Navel, Sex, Basic, raise the Fire to penetrate Crown Chakra.

KR-4 to KR-9 : Boostering

Attunement			
Level	KR-1	KR-2	KR-3
Energy	Reiki	Kundalini + Reiki	Diamond Reiki
Technique	☐ Healing ☐ Distance Healing ☐ Cleansing Room ☐ Karmic Band Healing ☐ Situation Healing	☐ Kundalini Meditation	☐ Crystalline Reiki ☐ DNA Reiki ☐ Birth Trauma Reiki ☐ Location Reiki ☐ Past Life Reiki ☐ Balance ☐ Before Treatment ☐ Complete Treatment ☐ Master 1 Master 1 can

			provide Attunement of KR 1-2-3

Attunement		
Level	KR 4-5-6	KR 7-8-9
Energy	Gold Reiki 1-2-3	
Technique	☐ **Booster 1** ☐ **Master 1** Master 1 can provide Attunement of KR 1 to KR 6, and Gold Reiki 1 to 3	☐ **Booster 2** ☐ **Master 3** Master 3 can provide Attunement of all levels of KR and Gold Reiki

Kundalini Reiki Techniques

Kundalini Reiki 1

1. Healing

The energy channeling technique to heal a patient is performed by touching both palms on the patient's shoulders, and channeling the energy for about 3-5 minutes.

2. Distance Healing

Distance healing technique is performed by visualizing "the patient's name and body" in both palms and channeling the energy for about 3-5 minutes.

3. Cleansing Room/House

Room/house cleansing is performed by visualization (distance healing technique), channeling the energy for about 3-5 minutes.

Do it regularly every 14 days.

4. Healing The Carmic Band

This technique aims to improve relationship between a person and another.

This is performed by intending for the relationship to be harmonized or by the writing release technique, which is to write down the situation to be realized into the palms (virtually).

5. Situation/Qualities Healing

This technique aims to improve the bad condition or human bad nature. This technique is similar to Karmic Healing.

Kundalini Reiki 2

- **Kundalini Reiki**

  Every time you intend "Kundalini Reiki", the channeled energy is a combination of Reiki and Kundalini energies.

- **Kundalini Reiki Meditation**

  It is performed by intending "Kundalini Reiki Meditation", without the need for visualization.

  For novice practitioners, it is performed for 5 minutes and only once a day. After the body adjusts to the energy, they can increase the duration and amount of energy.

Kundalini Reiki 3

1. Diamond Reiki

It is performed by intending "Diamond Reiki", then an etheric crystal (diamond) will be in the Crown Chakra of the practitioner, and strengthen the quality of Reiki channeled by the practitioner.

Please observe the different types of energy of Diamond Reiki!

2. Crystalline Reiki

There are fine grains of crystals in the human body, where these crystals are places of "recording" of various traumas (due to certain events).

The Crystalline Reiki technique is a method to cleanse the "recording" of the traumas. It can be activated by intending "Crystalline Reiki", then channeling the energy by touching the patient's body.

It is conducted in 2 sessions, each session is 15 minutes long. This technique cannot be performed at a distance.

3. DNA Reiki

This technique is used to improve the quality of human DNA, and it takes 3 weeks after the treatment process for the effect.

It can be activated by intending "DNA Reiki", then channeling the energy for 3-5 minutes. This technique can be performed at a distance.

Kundalini Reiki 3

1. Birth Trauma Reiki

One form of trauma is a trauma due to "birth process".

This trauma can be healed gradually using this technique. It can be activated by intending "Birth Trauma Reiki", then channeling the energy for 3-5 minutes.
This technique can be performed at a distance.

2. Location Reiki

This technique is used to harmonize "The Carmic Band" between human and a location or place (this karma string can interfere with health or other things).

For example, between a person and a place with full of negative energy (hospital, grave, etc.).

It can be activated by intending "Location Reiki", then channeling the energy for 3-5 minutes.

This technique can be performed at a distance.

3. Past-Life Reiki

This technique is to eliminate blockage occurring in the past lives (for those who believe it).

It can be activated by intending "Past Life Reiki", then channeling the energy for 3-5 minutes.

This technique consists of 3 sessions and can be performed at a distance.

4. Balance Reiki

This technique is used to balance the entire body's energy system.

Meet the tips of the fingers and thumbs, then activate the technique by intending "Balance Reiki" for 30 seconds. This process will last for 1 hour. For a maximum process, it must be performed once a day.

Before Treatment

Before performing serious Reiki Treatment to others, a Kundalini-Reiki healer is advised to conduct a series of self-treatment consisting of: Crystalline Reiki, DNA Reiki, Location Reiki, Past-Life Reiki, and Birth Trauma Reiki (the duration of each treatment is about 1 minute).

Kundalini Reiki 4-5-6

- **Gold Reiki**

  Gold Reiki transforms "Fear" and "Gloom" into "Enlightenment" and "Happiness". This energy is the strongest energy in the physical realm. It can be used alone or combined with ordinary Reiki techniques. It can be activated by intending "Gold Reiki", then channeling the energy for 3-5 minutes. This energy can be channeled at a distance.

Attunement Techniques

Attunement techniques of Kundalini Reiki/Kundalini Reiki Booster/Gold Reiki

Preparation

The practitioner prepares the attunement by praying and meditating to connect with Kuthumi or Spiritual Masters.

The preparation lasts for 25 minutes.

Give affirmation: With the permission of God Almighty, I give an Attunement of: _____ to: _____, where the Attunement will be conducted on/at:_____ until finish, completely.

This affirmation lasts for 30 seconds.

The Attunement can be performed on an object (for example, a crystal).

The minimum age recommendation is 8 years!

Time Interval of Attunement

KR 1		
KR 2	2 days	→
KR 3	10 days	→
KR 4	Gold Reiki 1	2 days	→
KR 5	Gold Reiki 2	2 days	→

KR 6	Gold Reiki 3	5 days	→
KR 7		5 days	→
KR 8		5 days	→
KR 9		5 days	→

Simultaneous Attunement can be performed for granting rights, followed by re-attunement.

Gold Reiki is optional and can be provided with KR 4-5-6.

Conclusion

My dear readers

Hopefully after you read this book carefully, you can understand a fundamental way.

If you still do not understand very well, I recommend not to get bored to repeat it again from the beginning and try to it.

Try to understand what is implied by what you read, to the core of this book can be absorbed completely.

If I may share with readers, I have never read a book that I am interested in is less than three times, in fact there are books that I read up to 5 times.

Not because I do not understand the grammar, but because I wanted to deep understand "spirit" of the writing itself until I can animates without the need to memorize it word for word.

But of course, what I say is simply a reference to encourage the reader to never read only with the eyes alone but reading it with the mind, especially the heart.

Until the core of every book you read will be etched in your heart.

The key to be able to read well is, "*do not just read with the eyes and mind, but use with heart*"

Hopefully this simple book is able to provide meaningful knowledge for the world community, not just as a vehicle for supplementary reading, but more than that.

But so much hope must not turn a blind eye deficiencies contained in this simple book.

Therefore, suggestions and criticism from readers will i receive with all humility.

Therefore,
I understand that people are not willing to accept criticism, then he will never be successful.

May blessing everyone who reads the this book guided to attain self-enlightenment and knowledge of humans making wise and prudent and successful in life Greetings from my prayer,

*Elfitri (*illustrator and a Master Reiki from Lineage Yan Nurindra)
Waffa Z (Editor)

Nb : This book based on a knowledge from Master Reiki Usui with some changes follow the Western tradition

Bibliography

Baker, Douglas, DRF and Celia Hansen, *In Steps of The Master*, Little Elephant, 1977

Benson, H. *The Mind/Body Effect*, New York, Simon & Schuster

Roberts, Jane, *How to Develop Your ESP Power*, Frederik Fell Inc, 1966

Schoenmaker, Rev. Mario. *The New Clairvoyance*, Interbook Inc, 1986

Swami Satprakashnanda, *Meditation,* Sri Ramakrishna Math, Mylapore, Madras 600 004

Nurindra, Yan. Usui Reiki, Reikiasia.com (archive 2015)

Elfiky, Ibrahim. The Power of Thinking. Ibrahim Elfiky International Enterprises Inc

Efendi, Irmansyah. Soul Awareness, GM, 1999

Lobzang Zopta, Zen Reiki, Mediantara, 2011

A Glossary of Reiki related Terms

A

Advanced Reiki Training (ART)
Sometimes referred to as Level 3a, or as Master-Practitioner Level. In Usui/Tibetan Reiki the common Level 3 is separated into two parts. ART, i.e.
Level 3a focuses on 'personal mastery' and incorporates 'non-traditional' elements such as Reiki (crystal) grids, Psychic Surgery, Reiki Guide Meditations, healing attunements, the Antahkarana symbol, and meditation on the Reiki symbols. At this level the student receives the Level 3 ('Master' level) attunement, but is not instructed in the process of passing attunements to others.

Ai-Reiki
The state of being in harmony with Reiki

Anshin Ritsumei (also: Dai Anjin)
a state in which ones mind is totally at peace - not bothered by anything - and in which one perceives one's life's purpose

Antahkarana
A 'non-traditional' Reiki symbol, the Antakarana is a cube symbol, with an 'L' shape on each of its surfaces. The Antakarana is claimed to be a symbol of Tibetan origin, but there does not seem to be any proof of this.
Antakarana is said to be a panacea for all ills.

Aoki, Huminori (or Fuminori)
Huminori Aoki is Chairman of the Nagoya Reiki Lab (formerly the "Human & Trust Institute"), where he teaches his own form of Reiki, known as: Reido Reiki, a system which attempts to unite Western and Japanese Reiki Traditions.

Attunement (also: Initiation or empowerment)
The central focus of each Level or Degree - The sacred process performed by a Reiki Master (Teacher) essentially

re-patterns or recalibrates the students etheric field & subtle energy centres, enabling them to interact with the phenomenon that is Reiki. Called denju in Japanese.

B

Beaming
A non-contact method of giving Reiki treatment. Differs from distant treatment in that the client is actually present (i.e. within line-of-sight). The practitioner stands a short distance from the client and 'beams' or projects Reiki to them

Blue Kidney Breath
See: Breath of the Fire Dragon

Breath of the Fire Dragon
A special breathing technique used in Raku Kei Reiki. A variation of this practice, used in Tera Mai, is referred to as the Violet Breath. Yet another version is called the 'blue kidney breath'

Byogen Chiryo-ho
'Treating the root cause of a disease' [byo (disease) gen (root/origin) chiryo (treatment)] - a technique similar to Genetsu-ho

Byosen Reikan-ho
Also simply called Byosen. A Reiki technique in which the practitioner moves their hands through the client's aura/energy-field, sensing for energetic fluctuations - in particular, the 'energetic sensation' perceived at areas of dis-harmony or dis-ease. Referred to as 'Scanning' in 'western' Reiki styles.

However, Byosen is not solely concerned with energetic fluctuations. It is also about intuition or inspiration. The 'Reikan' part of the name is often translated as inspiration; though, in its deepest sense, Reikan refers more specifically to 'spiritual intuition ' - i.e. what we would probably understand better as 'psychic sensitivity'.

C

Chakra Kassei Kokyo-ho
Chakra-activating breathing method from Gendai Reiki Ho

CKR
See: Choku Rei

Choku Rei (or: Chokurei)
Name of the first of the four Usui Reiki symbols.
Commonly called the 'Power' symbol in Takata-lineage
Reiki (Usui Shiki Ryoho). In some Japanese lineages the
symbol is commonly called the 'Focus' symbol'.
Takata-Sensei translated Choku Rei as 'put the [spiritual]
power here', yet it can also translate as something akin
to: 'in the presence of the Spirit(s)' or even as 'Direct
Spirit'

Chuden
'Second / Middle (Chu) Teaching (Den)'. In some styles of
Reiki, a level of training between Shoden and Okuden

Chu Tanden (see: Tanden)
An energy 'centre' or area located deep inside the chest.
Crystal Grid

A particular geometrical layout of crystals that have been
charged with Reiki, designed to continually emanate
therapeutic or protective influence.

D

Dai Ko Myo
Name of the last of the four Usui Reiki symbols.
Commonly called the 'Master' symbol in Takata-lineage
Reiki (Usui Shiki Ryoho).
The ' symbol' is actually the words Dai, Ko, & Myo written
in kanji, and name literally means: 'Great Shining Light' -
signifying 'Enlightened Nature' or 'the Radiant Light of
Wisdom' the Radiance of a Deity (Buddha, Bodhisattva,

'Vidyaraja', etc) the manifest expression of the Light of Wisdom: the means by which illumination "dawns on us."

Dai Shihan (see: Shihan)
A term used (in some Japanese Reiki styles) to denote a level above that of Shihan (teacher/master). In these styles, one must attain the level of Dai Shihan in order to be allowed to initiate students to Shihan level. Dai Shihan is sometimes translated as 'Grand Master'.

Dashu-ho
Another term for Uchite Chiryo-Ho

Den
'Teachings' - this term is found in the titles of the grades or levels used in most Japanese Reiki traditions - e.g. Sho-den, Oku-den, Shinpi-den

Denju (see: Attunement)
'Initiation' - the 'Western' style Reiki attunement process used by Takata-Sensei. Denju refers to 'initiation' in the fullest sense of the word - including the energetic 'attunement', but also the teachings accompanying it.

Dento Reiki (-Ryoho)
'Traditional Reiki' - a term used by some to indicate Usui Reiki Ryoho

Distant Attunement
The (non-traditional) practice of performing a Reiki attunement on a student who is not physically present at the time. Most 'Japanese' styles of Reiki - e.g. Gendai, Komyo, Hekikuu, etc do not condone the practice of distant attunements (denju) or distant reiju.

As Kenji Hamamoto – founder of Hekikuu Reiki says:
"To effectively assist the student to awaken to Reiki, the teacher needs to be present, needs to be able to watch for the physiological signs that the process is actually unfolding; to receive tangible energetic feedback. It would

be disrespectful to the student to merely raise the hands at a distance, take their money, and hope."

Distant Symbol
See - Hon Sha Ze Sho Nen
Distant (also: Remote) Treatment
Process of performing a Reiki treatment for a client who is not physically present at the time.

DKM
See: Dai Ko Myo

Do
A (philosophical or spiritual) 'Path' or 'Way'

Dojo
'The Place of the Way' - while commonly used to refer to a Martial Arts Training Hall, the term originally referred to a place for Meditation and the pursuit of Spiritual Discipline. Usui sensei's Training Centre was referred to as a dojo.

Dumo
'Tibetan' Master Symbol' - as used in Raku Kei Reiki and several other modern styles of Reiki

E

Eguchi te-no-hira Ryoji
A hand/palm healing modality developed by Toshihiro Eguchi

Eguchi, Toshihiro
A friend and student of Usui Sensei, in 1930 Toshihiro Eguchi published: Te-no-hira Ryoji Nyumon (An Introduction to Healing with the Palms) and later, in 1954: Te-no-hira Ryoji Wo Kataru (A Tale of Healing with the Palms of the Hands).

Empowerment
See: Attunement
'Energy Exchange'

The concept that client (or student) must give something to the Practitioner/Teacher in recompense for the gift of treatment (or attunement) – as a sign of their appreciation, and also as an acknowledgement of the value of the Reiki gift. This can be a payment in cash or 'kind'. Originally intended to invoke the healing emotion of Kansha (gratitude) in the recipient, unfortunately some money-oriented Reiki folk now use this as an excuse for charging high fees.

Enkaku Chiryo-Ho
'Remote (Distant) Healing Method'

F

Finishing Stroke (also: Nerve Stroke)
Usui Shiki Ryoho Level 2 technique; essentially the same as Ketsueki Kokan-Ho

Fire Serpent
A symbol used in Raku Kei Reiki and several other modern styles of Reiki. Said to represent the kundalini energy residing in the spine. Also known as Nin Giz Zida

Fukuju (or: Fuku Ju)
A phrase used by some as the jumon (mantra) for the mental-emotional symbol.
Also the name of a well-known brand of Sake!
The phrase translates as: "a long & happy Life" or more loosely: "Cheers!"

G

Gainen
'Concepts' – a term used in Usui-do to refer to the Reiki Principles/Percepts

Gakkai
A 'Learning Society' - such as the Usui Reiki Ryoho Gakkai

Gassho

A ritual gesture formed by placing the hands together in a prayer-like position in front of the mouth - the fingertips at a level just below the nose. 'Gassho' implies recognition of the oneness of all beings. This gesture is also used to show reverence to Buddhas, Bodhisattvas, Patriarchs & Teachers

Gassho Kokyu-Ho
'Gassho Breathing Method' - the practice of 'breathing' through the hands while in the Gassho position

Gassho Meiso
Gassho Meditation

Ge Tanden (see: Tanden)
Another term for the: Seika Tanden - an energy 'centre' or area located deep inside the hara (belly/abdomen).

Gedoku-Ho
Detox technique - one hand is placed at seika tanden, the other on the lower back at approximately the same level.

Gendai Reiki Ho
'Modern Reiki Method' - modern form of Japanese Reiki created by Hiroshi Doi - combines some traditional Usui teachings & techniques with teachings & techniques from other energy-healing arts

Genetsu Ho
Technique used to reduce high temperature / bring down a fever

Gokai
The Five Reiki Principles / Precepts / Ideals

Gokai Sansho
Recitation of the Five Reiki Principles / Precepts (sansho here refers to 'three times')

Gokui Kaiden
Teacher Level in the Gendai Reiki Ho system of Reiki

Grand Master (see: Dai Shihan)
A title created by the Reiki Alliance to refer to the head of the organization.
Alternatively, a loose translation of a term (used in certain Japanese Reiki styles) for one authorised to initiate Reiki 'Masters'

Group Reiki
See: Shu Chu Reiki

Gumonji ho
The Morning Star meditation. It is claimed by some that Usui-sensei was undertaking this particular Buddhist meditation when he received the 'Reiki experience' on Kurama Yama. [There is however nothing to support the claim.]

Gyosei (Also: Meiji Tenno Gyosei)
Poetry penned by the Meiji Tenno (Emperor), about 125 of which are recited / sung at meetings of the Usui Reiki Ryoho

Gakkai
[These poems are in a style known as waka]

Gyoshi-Ho
'Gazing Method' - technique of healing with the eyes

H

Hado Kokyu-Ho
Breathing technique which involves intoning the sound 'Haa' while exhaling. Used for inducing relaxation; said to raise ones vibrational levels and enhance functioning of the immune system.

Hado Meiso Ho
Hado-breath meditation (a Gendai Reiki Ho technique)

Hand Positions

In the different styles of Reiki numerous different sets of hand placement positions are used in giving Reiki treatment. Some sets have as many as twenty positions, and some as few as five.

Hanshin Chiryo-Ho
'Half-body Treatment Method'

Hanshin Koketsu-Ho
'Half-body Blood-purifying Method' - a version of Ketsueki Kokan-Ho

Hara
'Belly' - the extended area between the top of the pubic bone and the base of the sternum. In Japanese thought, hara is the seat of the individual's ki - their vital power.

Hara Chiryo ho
See: Tanden Chiryo Ho

Hatsu-rei-Ho
Generate[/Invoke] (Hatsu), Spirit (Rei), Method (Ho) - a set of primarily Ki-jutsu techniques which Usui Sensei is said to have taught as an aid to self-development. However there is a good possibility that Hatsurei-Ho was originally intended to be used solely as a ritual during which the student received reiju.

Hayashi, Chujiro
(1880 – 1940) retired Commander, Japanese Naval Reserve, Medical Doctor, and student of Usui sensei.
In 1930, Chujiro Hayashi began to modify his approach to Reiki (presumably to bring it more in line with his own understanding of clinical methodology/practice) and went on to establish the Hayashi Reiki Ryoho Kenkyukai.

Healing Crisis (also: Koten Hanno)
A temporary, cathartic or abreactive response which some individuals may experience as part of the healing process. (Many people never experience this at all)
'Healing Space', the (see: 'Holding the Healing Space')

Hekikuu Reiki
Hekikuu ('Azure Sky') Reiki is the name given by Kenji
Hamamoto to his personal 'understanding and expression'
of the therapeutic art, based on almost two decades of
practice. Hekikuu Reiki strongly informed by elements of
Japanese 'Folk Spirituality'.

Heso Chiryo-Ho
Acupressure-type energy-balancing technique applied to
the navel with middle finger.
Considered to have a beneficial on the kidneys

Hibiki
'Reverberation' - sensation in the hands, the nature of
which can indicate the presence and status of a dis-ease

Hikari no Kokyu-Ho
'Breath of Light' Method - a variant of Joshin Kokyo-Ho

Hikkei
'Companion' - a handbook or manual

Ho
'Method' or 'Technique'

Ho
A term used in Gendai Reiki to refer to the Reiki Symbols
'Holding the Healing Space'
Term referring to the whole process of facilitating the
client's 'opportunity for healing' - the creating and
maintaining ('holding') of a suitable environment - not so
much the physical environment as the emotional and
energetic 'environment': a safe and relaxing psychological
'inner space' in which the individual can heal themself with
Reiki's assistance

Hon Sha Ze Sho Nen (or: Hon Ja Ze Sho Nen)
Name of the third of the four Usui Reiki symbols.
Commonly called the 'distant' symbol in Takata-lineage
Reiki (Usui Shiki Ryoho). [However, in some 'Japanese'

styles of Reiki -Hekikuu Reiki for example - Hon Sha Ze Sho Nen is not taught as a 'distant' symbol but rather as one pertaining to the mental faculties.]

This ' symbol' is actually the words: Hon, Sha, Ze, Sho, & Nen, written in kanji (albeit in a stylized form). While some people have sought to translate the phrase Hon Sha Ze Sho Nen 'as: "no past, no present, no future", this mantra phrase more clearly translates as: 'Correct Thought (Correct Mindfulness) is the essence of Being'

HSZSN
See: Hon Sha Ze Sho Nen

I

Ibuki Ho
Breath technique

Independent Reiki Masters
A term originally coined to refer those masters who did not belong to either the Reiki Alliance or the American Reiki Association, Inc, but rather preferred to 'go their own way'.

In-Yo
Equivalent of the Chinese Yin-Yang

J

Jaki Kiri Joka Ho
Technique for 'energetic cleansing' of inanimate objects. NOT to be used on living things: people, plants or animals [This technique seems to be derived from a more involved practice called the 'Ki Barai']

Japanese Reiki (see also: Western Reiki)
Term intended to refer to styles of Reiki which have evolved in Japan - as distinct from those based on the Usui Shiki Ryoho teachings of Takata sensei (several of which have been imported into Japan from the West).

However the lines become somewhat blurred as several styles of Reiki classed as 'Japanese' [i.e. Vortex, Reido, Gendai, Komyo, Shinden] are actually a blending of both 'Japanese' and 'Western' teachings and practice.

Jikiden Reiki
'Original Teaching' or 'Directly Taught' Reiki - Japanese Reiki System now taught by Tadao Yamaguchi whose mother, Chiyoko Yamaguchi, was a student of Chujiro Hayashi

Jiko Joka Ho
A Gendai Reiki Ho self-purification practice

Jisshu Kai
Training/Practice Meetings

Jo Tanden (see: Tanden)
An energy 'centre' or area located in the middle of the head between the eyes

Joshin Kokyo-Ho
Cleansing Breathing technique used to stimulate, strengthen and purify the flow of Reiki (- a variant of Hikari no Kokyu-Ho) - a component of Hatsurei-Ho

Jumon
A 'Spell' - a Mantra or Sacred Invocation. Term commonly used to refer to the name accompanying each Reiki symbol (e.g: Choku Rei, Hon Sha Ze Sho Nen, etc.) indicating that the name is also the symbol's mantra. However, in some schools/styles of Reiki, some of the symbols have been given an alternative name, and also a separate jumon (mantra) which is intoned in place of the symbol name.

K

Kaicho
A president / chairman - title of the leader of the Usui Reiki Ryoho Gakkai

Kami Tanden (see: Tanden)
An energy 'centre' or area located in the middle of the
head between the eyes

Kanji
Chinese characters used for writing Japanese

Kanboku
A term used to indicate the Reiki symbols by Yuji Onuki -
a student of Toshihiro Eguchi [see also shirushi]

Kantoku
Illuminating visionary mystical state - brought about by
practice of strict ascetic mystical disciplines including
fasting, isolation, meditation & the use of incantation and
mudra-like techniques

Karuna Ki
'Compassionate Heart Energy'. A Reiki style developed by
Vincent (Vinny) Amador based on Tera Mai and Karuna
Reiki, with additional elements based on Raku Kei Reiki
practice

Karuna Reiki
Style of Reiki developed by William Lee Rand and the
International Center For Reiki Training, based primarily on
Sai Baba Reiki

Kawamuru, Hawayo
See: Takata, Hawayo

Kenyoku-Ho
'Dry Brushing Method' - essentially an aura-cleansing
technique - a component of Hatsurei-Ho

Kenkyu kai
Term for meetings held by the Usui Reiki Ryoho Gakkai

Kenzon no Gebri

'Health Principles' - title of a book by a Dr. Bizan (or Miyama) Suzuki. A 1915 edition of this book includes the admonition:
"Just for today, do not anger, do not fear, work hard, be honest, and be kind to others."
This is almost certainly the direct source of Usui Sensei's Five Reiki Principles or gokai

Ketsueki Kokan-Ho
'Blood Exchange Technique' - actually refers to a blood-cleansing technique. A version used in 'western' style Reiki is often called the 'Finishing' or 'Smoothing' technique or 'Nerve Stroke'

Kihon Shisei
(Foundation / Standard Posture) Refers to the starting position in Hatsu Rei Ho - ideally, sitting in traditional Japanese seiza posture, eyes closed, with attention focussed in the seika tanden

Ki-jutsu
'Energetic Arts' - Collective term for Japanese disciplines concerned with the development, strengthening and refinement of 'Ki'

Kikai Tanden (See: Tanden)
Another term for the: Seika Tanden - an energy 'centre' or area located deep inside the hara (belly/abdomen).

Ki Ko
A (modern) Japanese name for the Chinese Art of Chi Gung (Qi Gong)

Kiriku
Pronounced somewhere between: k'rik and k'lik - the 'spiritual emblem' of Amida Butsu, and probable origin of the second of the four Usui Reiki symbols - Sei Heiki

Koketsu-Ho
'Blood-purifying Method'

Koki-Ho
'Exhalation (Koki) Method' - technique of healing with the breath
[note: not the same as koki ('second term') as used in Okuden-koki]

Kokiyu-ho
Breath-empowerment method. A Usui Shiki Ryoho technique used to empower the breath when giving attunement. Sometimes referred to as 'sweetening the breath'.

Kokoro
Heart, Spirit, Will, Mind

Kokyo-Ho (or: Kokyu-ho)
Breathing techniques for development, strengthening and purification of ki

Komyo Reiki
Style of Reiki developed by Hyakuten Inamoto - based on Jikiden Reiki, which Inamoto learned from Chiyoko Yamaguchi. Komyo Reiki places emphasis on personal spiritual transformation - that is: 'Satori' - through Reiki practice, and holds that Usui-Sensei's original teachings focussed on spiritual development, and that any healing that took place was merely considered a side effect to this spiritual growth.

Koriki
A 'non-traditional' symbol and mantra taught at level 1 in Reido Reiki. Koriki is referred to as the 'force of happiness' or 'power of happiness'. Said to grant peace and serenity.

Koriki
A Buddhist term, referring to 'spiritual power' or 'meritous power' accrued via practice of various ritual, meditative, or venerative disciplines such as ajikan (meditation on the siddham 'A' character), nembutsu (chanting the 'Namu Amida Butsu'), nyorai kaji, shugyo asceticisms, etc, etc.

[This 'koriki' is not written in the same kanji as the 'koriki' used in Reido Reiki]

Koshin-do Mawashi
The 'Reiki Circle' method. [also called Reiki Mawashi]

Koten Hanno
See: Healing Crisis

Kotodama
'Word-Spirit' - a multi-faceted discipline originating within Shinto, a primary element of which involves the intoning of sacred sounds (both syllables and individual vowel-sounds)

Kumo
'Cloud' - A word used by some as the name for the 'power' symbol. Also see: Un ['Kumo' and 'Un' are two different 'readings' of, or ways of pronouncing, the same kanji character] Also see: Zui-un

Kurama Yama
Horse-saddle (Kurama) Mountain (Yama) - the Sacred Mountain where Usui-Sensei is believed to have first experienced Reiki

L

Leiki
There is no true 'R' sound in Japanese. The actual sound identified by 'R' in 'Reiki' is a sort of a blending of 'R' & 'L'. In her diaries, Takata Sensei does not write the word as 'Reiki', but rather as 'Leiki'.
'Leiki: a Memorial to Takata-sensei'
See: 'Gray Book'

Lineage (Reiki Lineage)
The list of ones 'Reiki Antecedents' – ones Reiki Teacher, ones teacher's Teacher, and so on, back to Usui-sensei

Lotus Repentance Ritual

It is claimed by some that Usui-sensei was undertaking this particular Buddhist ritual when he received the 'Reiki experience' on Kurama Yama. [There is however nothing to support the claim.]

M

Makoto no kokyu- ho
The "Breath of Sincerity" or "Breath of Truth" - a self-developmental exercise taught in some styles of Reiki with the intent of developing greater awareness of ones seika tanden (energy centre in the lower abdomen).
The practice, though claimed to be part of Usui-sensei's original teachings, has most probably simply been 'borrowed' from the art of Aikido at a relatively recent point in time.

Master Symbol
See: Dai Ko Myo

Meiji Tenno Gyosei
See: Gyosei

Mental-Emotional Symbol
See: Sei Heiki

Menkyo Kaiden
A Teacher's Licence - certification of achievement of the highest levels of proficiency in a given art. Usui sensei is said to have gained Menkyo Kaiden in the martial discipline of Yagyu Ryu

Mitsui, Mieko
Journalist and Reiki Practitioner. The first person to teach Western style Reiki in Japan, Mieko could be said to have been responsible for single-handedly sparking a Japanese 'Reiki Revival'.

Mochizuki, Toshitaka
Toshitaka Mochizuki published "Iyashi No Te" in 1995 (- believed to be the first modern day Reiki book written by

a Japanese master). Mochizuki attributes some of the historical information presented in his book to an obscure Japanese book entitled "The Secret of How to Take Care of Your Family Members" by Takichi Tsukida.

Mokunen
(Focusing) an element of Hatsu Rei Ho

Mugen Muryouju (or: Mugen Muryo Ju)
As part of an attempt to 're-Buddha-fy' Reiki, in some Japanese styles of Reiki the SHK symbol has been renamed to either Muryouju or Mugen Muryouju. Muryouju is the Japanese name for Amida Butsu in his manifestation as 'Buddha of Infinite Life'. Mugen can refer to infinite compassion or infinite wisdom.

Muryouju (or: Muryo Ju)
See: Mugen Muryouju

N

Nade-Te Chiryo-Ho
Stimulating the flow of ki in the body by stroking with the hand

Naka Tanden (see: Tanden)
An energy 'centre' or area located deep inside the chest.

Nao Hi
An alternative name for Choku Rei. Both terms have the same meaning: 'Direct Spirit'

Nentatsu-Ho
A Level 1 technique, essentially a form of 'thought-transmission' via the hands. Used to 'realign' habits. A variation of nentatsu-ho taught at Level 2 is called seiheki chiryo ho.

Nerve Stroke (also: Finishing Stroke)
See: Ketsueki Kokan-Ho

Nin Giz Zida
Another name for Raku Kei Reiki's 'Fire Serpent 'symbol

O

Okuden
'Inner Teachings' - Level II in some versions of the Reiki grading system. Oku refers to the 'inner' the depths or heart of a thing - the esoteric or secret aspect of a thing.

Okuden Koki
In Reiki systems where the Okuden level is divided into two parts, the suffix -koki ('Second Term') is added to indicate the second part.

Okuden Zenki
In Reiki systems where the Okuden level is divided into two parts, the suffix -zenki ('First Term') is added to indicate the first part.

Oshite Chiryo-Ho
'Pressing Hand' - actually, an acupressure-type technique applied with the fingertips

P

Percepts
See: Gokai

Principles
See: Gokai

Power Symbol
See: Choku Rei

R

Radiance Technique, The
A Style of Reiki incorporating seven Levels or Degrees, promoted by Barbara (Weber) Ray. Ray claims that

Takata Sensei taught her this seven-degree system between 1978 and 1980.

Raku
A symbol from Raku Kei Reiki. Looking like an extended 'lightning-bolt', Raku is used at the conclusion of the attunement process to separate the energy/auras of teacher and student. Also used in Usui/Tibetan Reiki.

Raku Kei Reiki
Known as "The Way of the Fire Dragon" - Raku Kei is the creation of Reiki master Arthur Robertson (deceased). It uses additional symbols and claims a Tibetan origin for Reiki.

Re-attunement
See: Repeat Attunement

Rei
To Bow - as in: Sensei ni Rei - bow to ones teacher(s), or, Shinzen ni Rei - bow to a shrine. By bowing you are expressing respect, courtesy, and gratitude - to the person, concept or spiritual being you are bowing to, and also, to yourself.
[This 'rei' is not written in the same kanji as the 'rei' in 'Reiki']

Reido
'Spirit Movement' - involuntary bodily movement (eg. rocking or swaying). A form of cathartic response, sometimes triggered/stimulated by the application of Reiki and other energetic therapies.

Reido Reiki
A Japanese Reiki system which attempts to unite Western and Japanese Reiki Traditions, developed by Huminori Aoki, Chief of the Nagoya Reiki Lab (formerly the "Human & Trust Institute).

Reiho (also: Reishiki)
Etiquette; a method of bowing

Reiho
'Spiritual Method' -as in: Usui Reiho: Usui Spiritual Method
Some people claim that 'Reiho' is a contraction of: 'Reiki

Ryoho'
(Reiki Healing Method) This 'Reiho' is not written in the
same kanji as the 'Reiho' meaning Etiquette]

Reiji
'Indication of the Spirit' - Spiritual guidance in the placing
of your hands to give treatment

Reiju
Spiritual (Rei) Gift (Ju) - term for the original form of Reiki
Attunement-Empowerment

Reiki
The term commonly used to indicate the therapeutic and
self-development system created by Mikao Usui, and more
specifically, the wonderful therapeutic energy-radiance, or
phenomenon, which lies at the heart of this natural
healing system.
(However, the word 'Reiki' has, it seems, achieved generic
status, being used to refer to numerous hands-on healing
practices of unrelated origin.)
The term Reiki is often erroneously translated as meaning
'universal energy'. And while it can be translated in a
simplistic sense as: 'Spiritual Energy' or 'Spiritual Feeling';
it refers more directly to 'Spirit', 'Spirit Force', or 'Spiritual
Influence' - the effect of Spirit in action.
In some instances 'Reiki' can be used as a term for an
Ancestral Spirit. (See also: Reiki Consciousness)

Reiki Circle (also: Reiki Current)
See: Reiki Mawashi

'Reiki Consciousness'
Term that speaks to the perception that, while Reiki is
commonly (and perhaps somewhat superficially)
perceived as a form of therapeutic 'ki' or energy, at a

deeper level it can be experienced as a direct manifestation of Spiritual Presence. (Some believe it to be an expression of our own Spirit, some, the 'Universal' Spirit.)

Reiki Ethics
Guidelines for Reiki teachers and practitioners concerning professional conduct

Reiki (Crystal) Grid
See: Crystal Grid

Reiki Guides
Spirit Beings who are believed by many to attend and assist Reiki practitioners in giving treatments.

Reiki Ho
the 'Reiki Method (of healing)' - a term used by some to refer to Reiki healing in general. However, others use it more specifically to refer to Gendai Reiki Ho

Reiki Jutsu
Translates as 'Art of Reiki', however Reiki Jutsu is actually the name of a martial art (developed by Andy Wright) which combines elements of Reiki and Shotokan Karate!

Reiki Lineage
The chain of Reiki Teachers between any given practitioner and Usui-Sensei

Reiki-ka
A Reiki Practitioner

Reiki Marathon
See: Renzoku

Reiki Master
More properly 'Reiki Teacher' -someone who has not only received Master Level attunement and knows how to carry out the attunement process for all three levels, but has also taught at least one class and thus has actually

attuned at least one student. Technically refers to someone who is part of a Teacher - Student (Mentor - Student) relationship

Reiki Master Practitioner
Term used in Usui/Tibetan styles of Reiki to indicate a person who is at the Level 3a (see: Advanced Reiki Training).

Reiki Master Teacher
Term used in Usui/Tibetan styles of Reiki to indicate a person who is at the Level 3b - i.e. they have been shown the master symbol and the methods of passing Attunement / Initiation. (see: Advanced Reiki Training).

Reiki Mawashi
'Reiki Circle'. Also: Reiki Current A group-based energy cycling meditation.

Reiki Ryoho Hikkei
'Reiki Treatment Companion' - a 68 page, Level 1 (Shoden) manual given to students of the Usui Reiki Ryoho Gakkai. Comprises of a Q&A section & explanation of Reiki - supposedly in Usui Sensei's own words - a healing guide (Ryoho Shishin), & Waka Poetry penned by the Emperor Meiji. The 'Hikkei' was compiled in the 1970's by Kimiko Koyama, sixth kaicho of the Usui Reiki Ryoho Gakkai

Reiki Ryoho No Shiori
'Guide to Reiki Ryoho' - the title of a document compiled by two Gakkai presidents: Koyama & Wanami, said to be given to all members of the Usui Reiki Ryoho Gakkai. The 'Shiori covers the history & purpose of the Gakkai, and sets out its administrative system. It outlines the characteristics of Reiki Ryoho, deals with the how to strengthen Reiki, & includes a number of techniques such as: koketsu ho, byosen, nentatsu ho, etc. It also contains comments by mainstream Medical Practitioners, lists 11 of Usui-Sensei's shinpiden students; and instruction from Mikao Usui.

Reiki Ryoho To Sono Koka
Reiki Ryoho & Its Effects - title of a book written by Mataji
Kawakami in 1919.This book was not about 'Usui Reiki
Ryoho'.
It seems that the term Reiki Ryoho (indicating 'Spiritual
Healing') was used by several therapists, before Usui-
Sensei, to describe their practices.

Reiki Shower
An aura-cleansing/replenishing technique found in some
'western' styles of Reiki

Reiki Symbols
(see also: Shirushi & Kanboku)
Four 'tools' used in Reiki – According to Takata-sensei,
only three are for use by practitioners as part of giving
treatment; the fourth is reserved for use in passing
attunements.

Reiki Un-do
A method of Reiki treatment received through
spontaneous movement - albeit intentionally initiated.
This technique was introduced to the Usui Reiki Ryoho
Gakkai by the society's sixth kaicho: Kimiko Koyama.

"Reiki wa darenimo deru"
"Everyone can do* Reiki". book privately published in
1986, by Japanese Reiki Master Fumio Ogawa
[* Radiate / Emanate]

Renzoku
A 'Reiki marathon', or 'relay' treatment. A practice
wherein several practitioners take turns at providing Reiki
in a continuous treatment session – often over many
hours, even days – to a single client

Repeat Attunement
(also: Re-attunement)
Takata sensei taught that an attunement was permanent,
and it didn't 'fade', need 'topping up' or have an expiration

date. But after her death, several 'western' Reiki Masters began experimenting with the idea of 'repeat attunements'. The theory supposedly being that repeating the attunement process result in a 'deepening of the quality' of the students connection to Reiki.

Ryoho
'Healing Method; (Medical) Treatment' - as in: Usui Reiki Ryoho: Usui Reiki Treatment

Ryoho Shishin
A treatment guide, written by Chujiro Hayashi - very similar in content to the healing guide in the Reiki Ryoho Hikkei. Hawayo Takata is known to have had this guide and gave copies to some of her students. It was also included in the 'Gray Book' compiled by Alice Takata Furumoto

S

Sai Baba Reiki
An early expression of the Tera Mai system, developed by Kathleen Milner

Saibo Kassei Ka
A cell-activating/vitalizing technique from Gendai Reiki Ho

Saihoji Temple
A Jodo (Pure Land) Buddhist temple in Tokyo. Usui sensei's remains are interred in the temple graveyard. This is also the site of the Usui Memorial stone erected by members of the Usui Reiki Ryoho Gakkai

Scanning
See: Byosen Reikan-ho

Seichim Reiki
Style originating with Reiki Master Patrick Zeigler, who claims to have had a mystical experience in the Great Pyramid at Giza, and also received a spiritual initiation from a Sufi order in Egypt.

Seiheki Chiryo-Ho
(A variant form of Nentatsu-Ho) Seiheki Chiryo-Ho is taught at Level 2 and makes use of symbols where Nentatsu-Ho does not.

Sei Heiki (or: Sei Hei Ki)
The second of the four Usui Reiki symbols: commonly called the 'mental/emotional' symbol in Takata-lineage Reiki (Usui

Shiki Ryoho
In Japanese lineages the symbol is commonly called the 'Harmony' symbol'.
Depending on the kanji used to write 'Sei Heiki', the name can mean 'emotional calmness' or 'spiritual composure'

Seika no Itten
'The One Point below the Navel'. Another term for the: Seika Tanden

Seika Tanden
(see: Tanden)
Concept found in traditional Japanese disciplines - martial, spiritual or artistic. The seika tanden (commonly referred to simply as 'the tanden') is an energy 'centre' or area - perceived by some to be about the size of a grapefruit - located deep inside the hara (belly/abdomen), Seika refers to 'below the Navel'

Seikaku Kaizen-ho
"Character improvement method" - alternative term for/version of, nentatsu ho

Seishin Toitsu
Contemplation ('Unification of mind/spirit') - an element of Hatsu Rei Ho

Seiza
Traditional Japanese kneeling posture, sitting back on (or between) the heels

Sekizui Joka Ibuki-Ho
Spinal Cord (Sekizui) Purification (Joka) Breath (Ibuki)
Method (Ho) - a technique of 'insufflation'

Sensei
Honourific form of address - as in 'Usui Sensei', 'Hayashi
Sensei', etc. Often translated as 'master' or 'doctor' but
more properly 'teacher'. A person should never add
'Sensei' to their own name when introducing (or speaking
about) themself

Shashin Chiryo ho
Distance-Healing Method using a Photograph
Shihan (also Shihan Sensei; Dai Shihan)
A Teacher or Instructor. More fully: "An expert who
teaches by example"
This term is used in Jikiden Reiki for the grade above
Shihan Kaku

Shihan Kaku
An Assistant Teacher or Instructor. Term used in Jikiden
Reiki for the grade above Okuden

Shihan Sensei
A Teacher or Instructor. Term used in Jikiden Reiki for the
grade above Shihan Kaku

Shiki
'Style' - as in Usui Shiki Ryoho: Usui Style Healing Method

Shimo Tanden
(see: Tanden)
Another term for the: Seika Tanden -an energy 'centre' or
area located deep inside the hara (belly/abdomen).

Shinpiden
'Mystery Teachings' - Level III (Master Level) in some
versions of the Reiki grading system

Shirushi

'Symbol' – see: Reiki Symbols; Kanboku

SHK
See: Sei Heiki

Shoden
'Elementary Teachings' - Level I in some versions of the Reiki grading system

Shu Chu Reiki
(also: Shudan Reiki)
Reiki treatment given to a single individual by a group

Shudan Reiki
Alternative term for a Reiki treatment given to a single individual by a group

Shuyo Ho
Group practice of Hatsu Rei Ho
T

Tanden Chiryo-Ho
(Also: Hara Chiryo Ho)
A body detoxification technique (similar to gedoku-ho)

Te-Ate
'Hand-Treatment' - generic term for Japanese hands-on healing modalities

Te no hira Ryoji Kenkyu Kai
Palm Healing Research Society - founded by Toshihiro Eguchi, a student of Usui Sensei.

Tera Mai
System developed from Reiki and Seichim by Kathleen Milner with the assistance of a 'Spiritual Being' (at one time taught to be the Indian spiritual master Satya Sai Baba)

Tibetan Master Symbol

A symbol used in Raku Kei Reiki and other modern styles. Also known as Dumo, this symbol is seen as the equivalent to the Dai Ko Myo used in more traditional Reiki styles.

Traditional Reiki
A term previously used to denote original Usui Shiki Ryoho practice as taught by Takata Sensei

Twenty one day cleansing process
Whereas some people may experience a healing crisis in response to receiving Reiki treatment, some students – on receiving attunement - may also experience similar yet less acute symptoms as their being adjusts to the changes brought about by the awakening of the phenomenon that is the Reiki ability (though many people never experience this at all). It is believed by some that this 'adjustment period' lasts for about 21 days (symbolically representative of Usui sensei's 21-day period of austerity on Mount Kurama?) and students are encouraged to self-treat with Reiki as much as possible during this time.

U

Uchite Chiryo-Ho
A Shiatsu-like patting or palpating technique

Un
'Cloud' - A word used by some as the name for the 'power' symbol. Also see: Kumo.['Kumo' and 'Un' are two different 'readings' of, or ways of pronouncing, the same kanji character] Also see: Zui-un

Un
A word used by some as the jumon (mantra) for the 'power' symbol. [Not to be confused with the other word Un, meaning Cloud] ['Un' is the Japanese pronunciation of the Sanscrit 'seed-syllable' mantra associated with the kami Maoson - one of the primary deities worshipped by the Kurama Kokyo sect on Mount Kurama]

Usui
A term used by many Japanese shamanic practitioners to describe 'power spots' - places where the 'veil' between this world and the World of the Spirit is thin. (Usui = Thin). However, in this instance, 'usui' -although having the same sound - is written in different kanji than the surname Usui

Usui Do
'Usui Way'. Term used to refer to Usui-sensei's original system of Spiritual Development. Also, a reconstruction of the original system, as taught by Dave King and the Usui Do Eidan.

Usui Kai
'Usui Society'. A modern term used to refer to the Usui Reiki Ryoho Gakkai

Usui, Mikao
Creator of the Usui Reiki system of healing and self development

Usui Reiki Ryoho
(see also Japanese Reiki)
'Usui Reiki Healing Method.' Term generally used to refer to Reiki as it evolved in Japan. Said to be closer to Usui-Sensei's original format. Utilizes Reiju rather than the symbol-centred attunements (denju) familiar in 'western' style Reiki. While generally using the term Usui Shiki Ryoho when speaking of Reiki, Takata sensei also occasionally used the term Usui Reiki Ryoho

Usui Reiki Ryoho Gakkai
'Usui Reiki Healing Method Learning Society'. While some say the society was founded by Usui-Sensei himself in 1922, it is generally accepted that the Gakkai was actually founded by Rear Admiral Juusaburo Gyuda (Ushida) and other students around 1926/7.

Usui Teate

Term used by some to refer to Usui-Sensei's Healing Method.
Also (confusingly) the name used to indicate teachings promoted by Chris Marsh and Andy Bowling as being an expression of Usui-Sensei's original system of Spiritual Development (as opposed to his Treatment Method). The term specifically means 'Usui Hand Treatment'.
NOTE: more recently, Dave King of Usui-do (see above) also began teaching 'Usui Teate', however this 'Usui Teate' is not the same as that taught by Chris Marsh...

Usui/Tibetan Reiki
Essentially a combination of Reiki as taught by Takata-Sensei and elements of Raku Kei Reiki. It makes use of both the standard Usui Reiki symbols and some Raku Kei symbols, plus numerous other 'non-traditional' elements. The third level is commonly separated into 3a and 3 b (see Advanced Reiki Training)

V

Violet Breath
A special breathing technique used in Tera Mai.
The Violet Breath is a variation of the Breath of the Fire Dragon technique found in Raku Kei Reiki.

Vortex Reiki
Modern Japanese style of Reiki, developed by Toshitaka Mochizuki, who had learnt Western style Reiki from Mieko Mitsui.

W

Waka
'Japanese Song/Poem' - short poems with lines containing fixed numbers of syllables. The Gyosei of the Meiji Emperor are in waka form. [The familiar Zen haiku are also a form of waka]
Western Reiki
Term used to refer to Reiki as taught in the West by Takata sensei, i.e. Usui Shiki Ryoho, and by extension, all

styles of Reiki based on Usui Shiki Ryoho. (see also: Japanese Reiki)

Y

Yagyu Ryu
Usui Sensei is believed to have achieved the high ranking of Menkyo Kaiden in Yagyu Ryu, a Bujutsu (Martial Arts) school focussing on the arts of Kenjutsu (swordsmanship) & Ju-jutsu (un-armed Combat) founded by Yagyu Muneyoshi Tajima no Kami (1527-1606).

Z

Zenshin Koketsu-Ho
'Full-body Blood Cleansing Technique' - a version of Ketsueki Kokan-Ho

Zui-un
While previously it was said that the Usui Reiki Ryoho Gakkai did not have names for the Reiki Symbols – that they simply referred to them as Symbol 1, Symbol 2, etc – it is now being claimed that they did have names for the symbols all along.
Supposedly they use the term Zui-un for the symbol commonly known as Choku Rei.
This use of Zui-un has also been adopted by some other schools/styles of Reiki.
Zui-un means: "Auspicious Cloud" – an omen of good luck. It is also the name of a popular brand of Japanese aloeswood incense. Also see: Un; and Kumo

Made in the USA
Coppell, TX
09 September 2024

36997021R00152